A Practical Guide to Career Learning and Development

D0218850

A Practical Guide to Career Learning and Development is an essential guide for all those involved in careers education, either with sole responsibility or as part of a team. With a focus on career happiness, resilience and growth, this exciting book offers effective pedagogical strategies, techniques and activities to make Career Learning and Development (CLD) accessible and enjoyable, contributing to positive outcomes for all young people in the 11–19 phase of their education.

With a wealth of support material such as teaching ideas, lesson plans and case studies, key topics covered include the following:

- CLD needs of young people
- CLD in the curriculum
- practical activities for age groups 11–14, 14–16 and 16–19
- creating a positive environment for learning
- teaching approaches
- leadership and management
- facilitating professional learning.

A Practical Guide to Career Learning and Development is an invaluable resource for careers advisers and staff in schools with responsibility for leading and providing careers education, as well as work-related learning, personal, social, and health and economic education (PSHEE), citizenship and pastoral programmes. It enables and supports all practitioners as they develop careers provision that better prepares young people for their future well-being and an ever-changing and unpredictable world of work.

Barbara Bassot is Senior Lecturer at Canterbury Christ Church University, UK, and Course Leader for the University Certificate in Understanding Careers Education and Guidance.

Anthony Barnes is an independent careers education consultant. He is also an honorary life member of the Career Development Institute and a fellow of the National Institute for Career Education and Counselling.

Anne Chant is Programme Director for the MA in Career Guidance at Canterbury Christ Church University, UK.

A Practical Guide to Career Learning and Development

Innovation in careers education 11–19

Barbara Bassot, Anthony Barnes
and Anne Chant

Routledge
Taylor & Francis Group

LONDON AND NEW YORK

First published 2014
by Routledge
2 Park Square, Milton Park, Abingdon, Oxon OX14 4RN

and by Routledge
711 Third Avenue, New York, NY 10017

Routledge is an imprint of the Taylor & Francis Group, an informa business

British Library Cataloguing in Publication Data
A catalogue record for this book is available from the British Library

Library of Congress Cataloging-in-Publication Data
A catalog record for this book has been requested

ISBN: 978-0-415-81645-8 (hbk)
ISBN: 978-0-415-81646-5 (pbk)
ISBN: 978-1-315-85092-4 (ebk)

Typeset in Galliard
by Apex CoVantage, LLC

Printed and bound in the United States of America by
Edwards Brothers Malloy

In memory of Chris Thomas, careers educator, whose life echoed the themes of this book

Contents

List of figures and tables   ix
Acknowledgements   xi
List of abbreviations   xiii
Introduction   xv

PART I
Preparing to teach Career Learning and Development (CLD)   I

1   **What is CLD?**   3
    Introduction 3
    The changing concept of career 3
    What is CLD? 5
    Career resilience 9
    Career happiness 12
    Career growth 15
    Conclusion 17

2   **Teaching for CLD**   18
    Introduction 18
    Supporting effective career guidance 18
    Creating a positive environment for learning 19
    Characteristics of effective career practitioners 20
    Teaching approaches 20
    Conclusion 36

3   **Curriculum development**   37
    Introduction 37
    CLD in the curriculum 37
    Curriculum leadership 41
    Strategic and long-term actions 41
    Resources and opportunities 48
    Middle management and medium-term actions 51
    Delivery and short-term actions 53
    Conclusion 56

PART II
Facilitating CLD   57

4   CLD 11–14   59
Introduction 59
Career resilience 59
Career happiness 65
Career growth 70
Conclusion 73

5   CLD 14–16   74
Introduction 74
Career resilience 74
Career happiness 79
Career growth 86
Conclusion 89

6   CLD 16–19   90
Introduction 90
Career resilience 90
Career happiness 95
Career growth 101
Conclusion 104

PART III
Developing your expertise in CLD   105

7   Leading and managing CLD   107
Introduction 107
Developing role clarity and clear role relationships 107
Developing policy 110
Your development as a leader of CLD 111
Leading improvements in careers teaching and learning 112
Facilitating the professional learning of all staff 113
Record keeping 116
Developing a communications strategy 120
Conclusion 121

References   123
Index   127

List of figures and tables

Figures

1.1	The CLD Bridge	6
1.2	Three key elements of the CLD Bridge	7
1.3	EFFE	8
2.1	A tutorial model for CLD	36
3.1	Students at the centre of the curriculum	55
4.1	Ahmed's network	62

Tables

1.1	The relationship between EFFE and career happiness, resilience and growth	9
1.2	What is needed for growth to occur	17
3.1	Progression in the areas of career and work-related learning from Key Stage 3 to P16	42
3.2	Template for CLD audit	45
3.3	Principal methods of data collection	50
3.4	Lesson schedule	52
7.1	Audit template	108
7.2	Outstanding careers teaching	112
7.3	Types of personal career records	117

Acknowledgements

We would like to thank our families and friends for their support in writing this book. In particular, we would like to thank Phil Bassot for his excellent work in producing the diagrams and Marc Bassot for his careful proofreading.

Figure 1.1 is used and adapted with kind permission from the Career Development Institute. It first appeared as 'Bassot (2009) Career Learning and Development: A Bridge to the Future', in the biennial research publication of the Institute of Career Guidance entitled *Constructing the Future; Career Guidance for Changing Contexts*, edited by Hazel Reid. It is available from http://www.icg-uk.org/ICG_publications.html.

Figure 1.2, B. Bassot, *The Reflective Journal*, 2013, Palgrave Macmillan, reproduced with permission of Palgrave Macmillan.

List of abbreviations

ACEG	Association for Careers Education and Guidance
CAD	Computer-aided design
CDI	Career Development Institute
CLD	Career Learning and Development
CV	Curriculum vitae
DfE	Department for Education
GCSE	General Certificate of Secondary Education
EFFE	Essential Foundation and Fundamental Entitlement
HE	Higher education
HR	Human resources
ICT	Information and communication technology
IT	Information technology
KS3	Key Stage 3
KS4	Key Stage 4
LMI	Labour market information
LO	Learning outcome (or objective)
LSIS	Learning and Skills Improvement Service
Ofsted	Office for Standards in Education Children's Services and Skills
P16	Post-16 education
PE	Physical Education
PSHE	Personal, Social and Health Education
PSHEE	Personal, Social, Health and Economic Education
QR	Quick response
VIA	Values in action
VLE	Virtual learning environment
ZPD	Zone of proximal development

Introduction

This book is written for all those who are involved in Career Learning and Development (CLD) and want it to be more relevant, creative and innovative. Preparing young people for turbulent labour markets and challenging working lives has never been more important. The days when most young people could leave school with a good curriculum vitae (CV) and get a job quickly and easily are long gone. Young people need to be positive, flexible and resilient to cope with the demands of working life, and effective programmes of CLD can do much to prepare them for what lies ahead. This book aims to equip you with the knowledge and skills you need to do this effectively; it gives you a wide range of creative ideas and points to a number of resources that can make CLD challenging and fun.

Towards the end of our first book, *An Introduction to Career Learning and Development 11–19*, we introduced the model of the CLD Bridge. This is a practical guide to show how this can be put into practice effectively with young people aged 11–19. Throughout the book, we focus on three aspects of the bridge – career resilience, career happiness and career growth – and present a range of activities and approaches that can be facilitated to enable young people to develop these vital skills and change their lives.

The book is divided into three parts. Part I, 'Preparing to teach Career Learning and Development (CLD)', begins by looking at what CLD is. The bridge model is revisited, and the three key themes of career resilience, happiness and growth are explored in some detail. Chapter 2 focuses on how CLD can be taught and assessed effectively, and Chapter 3 suggests practical approaches to curriculum design and development.

In Part II, 'Facilitating CLD', a wide range of activities and sessions are presented for students in particular age groups (11–14, 14–16 and 16–19). Chapters 4, 5 and 6 focus on the effective delivery of material that enables students to build career resilience, pursue career happiness and foster their career growth. These chapters contain a wealth of activities and suggestions for you to try.

In Part III, 'Developing your expertise in CLD', we consider a range of issues and strategies to enable the development of effective CLD within a learning organisation, such as a school or college. This includes the need for practitioners to develop themselves in their own role and to enable the development of their colleagues, both of which are vital to the delivery of high-quality CLD.

Throughout the book, case studies and examples are used to illustrate a range of issues. Some are imagined, and some are real; in the case of the latter, all names have been changed to preserve the anonymity of the people concerned.

We hope you will enjoy using this book and that it will help you towards your goal of helping young people build career resilience, achieve career happiness and continue in career growth.

Barbara Bassot
Anthony Barnes
Anne Chant

Part I

Preparing to teach Career Learning and Development (CLD)

Chapter 1

What is CLD?

Introduction

All young people need to be prepared for the world of work in the 21st century. In the past, it was sufficient to help them think about what they were going to do when they left school and to enable them to make an informed and realistic decision and to cope well with the transition from school to work. In today's changing and turbulent labour market, subject to the vagaries of the worldwide economy, this is no longer enough. Any decision regarding their future that young people make is likely to be the first of many such decisions that they will make during their adult life. For many people, the certainties of having a job in the long term and the feelings of security that this brings can no longer be taken for granted. Instead, we can expect to have to take control of our learning and development and manage our own careers.

The changing concept of career

The case study of 'Ruth' shows the experiences of an adult over the first few years of her working life. It illustrates something of what the future could hold for many young people.

RUTH

From an early age, Ruth enjoyed all kinds of artistic activities. Ruth was happy when she was painting and drawing at home or at school, making things or reading about how things were made. She decided to take art and design as one of her General Certificate of Secondary Education (GCSE) options, and when she chose her A levels, the only problem was which other subjects she would take with art as the rest came very much second choice. Ruth's A level in art helped her to develop her interests further, and she then went on to art college to do a foundation course. During her year at college, her interest in textiles emerged, and she applied to university to study for a degree in textiles for interiors.

As part of her degree course, Ruth spent three months in industry undertaking two unpaid placements, one working for a magazine and the other working in the textile design department of a well-known retailer. Here her love for all aspects of textile design was fostered. Ruth graduated with an upper-second-class honours degree and began to look for work.

Finding work in textile design for interiors proved extremely difficult. Ruth soon realised that there were many more jobs in fashion design (which do we buy more often, new clothes or new furniture and curtains?), and she knew she had to be more flexible in her outlook. She began to apply for a wide range of jobs in fashion and, after some searching, gained a job as a designer's assistant, working for a company making women's wear. The job was poorly paid, but fortunately, it was near to home. Ruth was frustrated as she was not involved in any aspect of the design process but learned an enormous amount about the production process. In her spare time, she undertook a little freelance work, and through this she continued to update her portfolio. Business was bad generally, and after just under a year, Ruth was made redundant.

After a short period of unemployment, Ruth's next job was again on the production side and again in fashion. Once more, she was frustrated with her lack of involvement in design but got to know some of the junior designers well. She realised by this time that she lacked some of the skills needed, particularly in computer-aided design (CAD), and was grateful when one of the designers offered to help her develop in this area in their spare time. She learned a lot from him and added the work she was doing to her portfolio. Ruth stayed with the company for a year, but times were still hard in the textiles sector, and she was made redundant again.

Ruth's next job, almost three years after graduating, was as a junior designer for a company that makes socks. She had never designed socks before, but she quickly progressed; she is now a designer, managing contracts for most of the stores in the United Kingdom where large numbers of people go to buy their socks. All of her sock designs are done on computer, but she always draws them by hand first, something that her clients particularly like as the end product is easier to visualise. She travels regularly to China and Turkey to visit the factories where her socks are made and then sees them in local stores at home.

You could argue that Ruth is now a long way away from her aspirations as a designer of textiles for interiors. However, her story shows that her journey was unpredictable, demanding a high level of resilience. She has become a designer, which contributes to her happiness, well-being and job satisfaction. This is something that many of her fellow students on her degree course failed to achieve, and she has needed to continue to develop her skills and talents in order to make herself marketable to employers and clients. Now in her early thirties, it is clear that she will need to continue to do this to progress, and even survive, in the highly competitive fashion industry.

Today's labour market makes many demands on young people. These include the following:

- Having a wide range of skills that can be transferred from one work situation to another as the need arises.
- Being flexible, adaptable and confident.
- Being well motivated and willing to continue to learn and develop the knowledge and skills required for the changing labour market.
- Being prepared to gain experience without necessarily being paid well (or even at all), especially in the early years of working life – good qualifications alone are no longer enough.

- Being prepared to continue to study whilst working, even if this means paying for it yourself and doing it on your own time.
- Being able to sell yourself to an employer.
- Having the determination to continue in the light of disappointment and rejection.

Young people at school are in the early days of their career development, and it would be wrong to expect them to be able deal with all of these demands effectively whilst still there. However, school can, and should, provide them with a safe and secure environment where they can practise their skills and build their knowledge in relation to career.

What is CLD?

In the past, most careers work was done by applying the matching model ('round peg in a round hole'). In our first book, *An Introduction to Career Learning and Development 11–19*, CLD was described as offering a different model with a distinctly alternative theoretical orientation. The metaphor of the CLD Bridge was used by Bassot (2009) and is built on the principles of social constructivism. For further information about the application of social constructivism to career guidance, see Bassot (2006). This approach argues that knowledge about career is not simply acquired by some kind of osmosis; people are not 'empty vessels' that can be 'filled up' with careers information, on the assumption that they can be advised or guided into making good decisions. By contrast, CLD asserts that knowledge about career is constructed through participation in activity and in interactions with a variety of people (including career professionals, employers, teachers, parents, peers and so on). Individuals (like Ruth) need ongoing experiences and opportunities for discussion in order to construct this knowledge within their changing social and cultural context. CLD happens not only when people are at school, but throughout their lives, as they continue to develop their knowledge and skills and adapt to the changing labour market.

CLD is important on three levels:

Individual – if people are happy and fulfilled at work they are more likely to achieve physical, emotional and mental well-being. Paid work is important in a basic financial sense, but it also gives people structure to their lives, provides a range of social relationships and forms part of a person's identity. Changing circumstances mean that people need to regularly revisit what is important to them and review the decisions they have made, and indeed need to continue to make throughout their lives.

Community – in our highly individualised society, work can be one of the few places where we feel that we belong to a community. We spend more time with the people we work with than most of the other people we know – even family and friends. In addition, CLD practitioners need to work with people within their own communities (e.g. employers, colleges, training providers and universities) in order to be able to offer a range of useful learning experiences to their students.

Social – work plays a vital role in maintaining social cohesion fostering well-being and promoting equality. High levels of unemployment can lead to high levels of dissatisfaction and isolation, low feelings of purposefulness and fulfilment and, for some, depression. CLD has a role to play in equipping people to deal with life's challenges and to challenge inequalities in society.

The CLD Bridge model revisited

In Chapter 11 of our first book, *An Introduction to Career Learning and Development 11–19*, we introduced the metaphor of the CLD suspension bridge as a way of describing how careers work needs to move forward in the future. Figure 1.1 shows the various aspects of the CLD Bridge; the bridge functions because of the tensions on opposing sides that keep it in balance.

The focus of this practical guide is to help you to understand how young people can learn to balance the pressures that they will experience as they construct their career. The left-hand side of the CLD Bridge focuses on the individual, and the right-hand side on society, often shown by the needs of employers and other stakeholders, and of governments who want to achieve their political goals. The elements of the bridge that we focus on in this book are shown in Figure 1.2.

They are as follows:

*   Career resilience
*   Career happiness
*   Career growth.

The issue of balance is of primary importance when considering the model of the CLD Bridge. The road (career growth) is supported by the anchorage blocks of career happiness on the left and career resilience on the right. If there is a lack of balance (e.g. all happiness and no resilience or vice versa), then the road collapses and there is no career growth. Programmes of CLD need to enable students to develop happiness and resilience and to

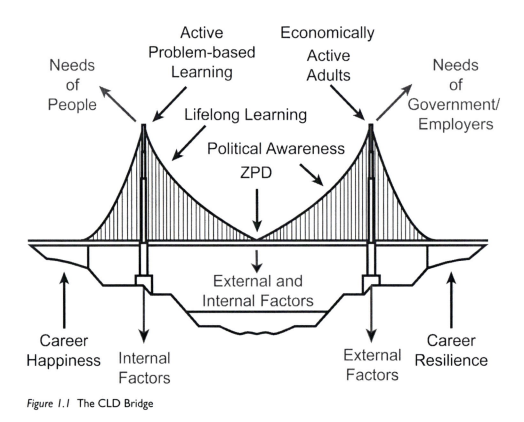

Figure 1.1 The CLD Bridge

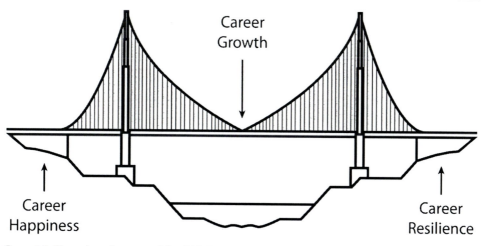

Career
Growth

Career
Happiness

Career
Resilience

Figure 1.2 Three key elements of the CLD Bridge

consider how they can keep these in balance so that career growth can happen. Each of the three elements is discussed in some detail in this chapter. At this point, it is worth spending a little time explaining two other key elements as shown in Figure 1.1.

- Active problem-based learning – in order to learn about career, young people need the opportunity to gain a range of experiences and to discuss them with others (teachers, tutors and peers). There is no substitute for experience, and all the activities in this guide are based on this premise. The notion of career is extremely abstract, and a lot needs to be done to help young people to learn in a more concrete way, particularly in the early years of secondary education. As they develop through secondary school, young people grow in their ability to think in an abstract way as they learn about themselves and the world around them. Even so, carefully designed activities can help them to consider a range of abstract issues and concepts.
- Lifelong learning – the case study of Ruth shows clearly that people need to continue to learn throughout their working lives in order to be able to adapt to their changing circumstances and the uncertainties of the labour market. CLD can foster a love of learning and can encourage those of all abilities and interests to take a keen interest in their own development.

Here, it is also important to emphasise that whilst we consider each of the three aspects (resilience, happiness and growth) separately, as concepts they are interdependent with some clear overlaps between them in evidence. For example, in general terms, career happiness relates to the inner life of the individual. It is made up of intense moments of pleasure and fulfilment as well as underlying feelings of contentment and well-being. Career growth, as illustrated by an individual's investment in lifelong learning, optimises the conditions for career happiness, whilst career resilience helps individuals to maintain a level of career happiness in adverse life situations.

Career growth relates to the progress made by individuals in learning and work. It is underpinned by deliberate planning and mere happenstance and is developed through significant learning relationships with career influencers. A determined outlook to strive for career happiness for oneself (and others) helps individuals to respond positively to a range of opportunities for career growth. Career resilience is not just about helping individuals to cope with the sometimes difficult tasks associated with career change, especially when unforeseen obstacles get in the way. It enables individuals to take advantage of unexpected opportunities for growth and development.

Career resilience relates to the staying power of individuals and their perseverance in overcoming obstacles, adapting to change and dealing with adversity. Developing and maintaining career happiness helps individuals to remain positive and to bounce back from difficult situations, for example by re-examining their personal values. Career growth provides the experiences and opportunities that enable individuals in time to recover from traumas and setbacks.

EFFE revisited

In the chapter on teaching and learning in our first book, we introduced the concept of Essential Foundation and Fundamental Entitlement (EFFE). This distillation of key theoretical elements and CLD programme content is a useful tool, not only to frame the development of a programme of learning, but also to evaluate a programme (see Chapter 3) and to map the interactive and interdependent nature of career learning.

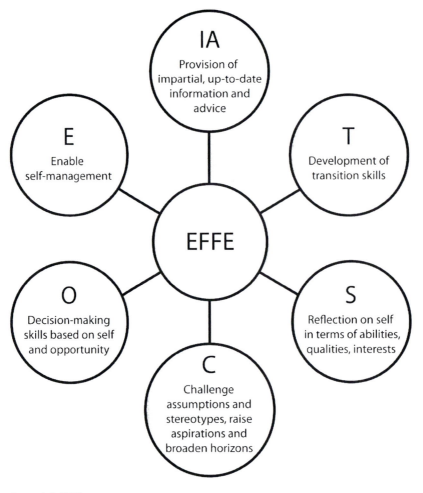

Figure 1.3 EFFE

Table 1.1 The relationship between EFFE and career happiness, resilience and growth

Elements of EFFE	Elements of the CLD Bridge		
	Career happiness	Career resilience	Career growth
Impartial advice and information	Impartial support reduces external pressures	Good understanding of options enables flexibility	Knowledge of progression routes
Transition skills	Facilitates successful transitions	Learning to process feedback from unsuccessful transitions	Improved confidence in transition and progression
Reflection on self	Recognition of own motivations and career essentials/anchors	Ability to reflect on learning from experiences	Confidence in decisions and ability to identify opportunities
Challenge assumptions	Broadening of opportunities beyond the traditional	Freedom from acceptance of stereotypical views of others	Widens horizons and encourages ambition
Make decisions about opportunities	Awareness of the criteria for choice, including values and interests	A well-established protocol for decision making, transferable to a range of transitions	Confidence in decision making and ability to take measured risks
Enable self-management	Being autonomous and self-sufficient	Confidence and control	Good planning and goal setting

As we consider the terms career happiness, resilience and growth, it is also useful to think about how these terms relate to the EFFE model. The above grid illustrates what can be achieved in terms of the three foci for this book within each of the elements of EFFE.

We now move on to examine each of the three key elements of the CLD Bridge in more detail.

Career resilience

The anchorage block on the right-hand side of the CLD Bridge represents career resilience. Before we can effectively grasp the concept of career resilience, it is helpful to look more broadly at resilience in other aspects of our lives. We all have skills, abilities and attributes, and what we experience and express in our careers cannot be disconnected from the rest of life; indeed our social lives, family life, work life and spiritual lives all have a dynamic interrelationship. The skills that we develop in one area of our lives are often realised in our approach to the world of work, and this principle is commonly at the heart of much of what we do in CLD in school. We encourage young people to think about the skills and qualities they have, their strengths and their attributes. We help them to see the possible relevance of this self-discovery in relation to the choices they make in education and in the world of work.

In this book, we make the same links regarding resilience. Career resilience, like other skills and attributes essential for effective career management, has its roots in our very earliest experiences of the ups and downs of life. The concept of resilience can be described as 'the ability to bounce back', to 'right oneself' and so relates to an event or experience that has had a negative or detrimental effect on a person and from which he or she has recovered. A definition of resilience is given in the subsequent box.

Resilience is

The process of self-righting and growth . . . The capacity to spring back, rebound, successfully adapt in the face of adversity, and develop social, academic and vocational competence despite exposure to severe stress or simply to the stress inherent in today's world.

Higgins (1994:373)

So, without the 'knock back' there can be no 'bounce back'. We learn that we can survive, manage and even benefit from adversity and thereby meet the next test stronger and with more self-belief and confidence.

Resilience can only develop through exposure to risk or to stress. Resilience develops through gradual exposure to difficulties at a manageable level of intensity and at points in the lifecycle where protective factors can operate.

Coleman and Hagell (2007:14)

In careers work there is a common discourse that teachers, career professionals, parents and young people themselves often articulate – 'I must not make the "wrong" decision.' Conversely, we could argue that unless young people are willing to risk making a choice that may not turn out the way they had intended, they will not learn the skills needed to make decisions more wisely in the future, although we would not advocate doing this deliberately, of course. The development of such resilience is essential in an ever more complex, competitive, global, rapidly changing and risky labour market. In this book, we argue that the place to develop career resilience, and the nurturing of the protective factors that can mitigate against the impact of risk, is within CLD.

These protective factors include those relating to the individual (confidence, strong relationships and academic ability), the family (supportive, accepting and encouraging) and the environment (the availability of opportunities or information and access to those opportunities). Poilpot (1999) classifies these factors into the following three areas that relate helpfully to CLD as follows:

- Personal strengths, feelings, beliefs and attitudes (**I am** . . . confident, popular, able).
- External resources and support (**I have** . . . people around me who care about me).
- Social and interpersonal competencies (**I can** . . . access the information and support I need).

In the subsequent box, six characteristics of resilience in younger children as identified by Wolin and Wolin (1993) are listed. The ability of a child to be creative and even funny (I am) is acknowledged as one of the indicators of resilience. Their ability to sustain relationships creates the external support needed (I have) to mitigate against adversity. The notion of risk is expressed within the notion of a child exploring his or her environment (I can).

Characteristics of resilience – Wolin and Wolin (1993)

1. Initiative – a child exploring his or her environment (I can).
2. Independence – ability to withdraw from an unpleasant circumstance or exhibit age appropriate autonomy (I am).
3. Insight – a child's sense that something is wrong with a situation (I am).
4. Relationship – a child seeking to connect with others, to form and sustain relationships (I have).
5. Humour and creativity – demonstrated in children at play (I am).
6. Morality – shown by a child's ability to judge right and wrong (I am).

Although the notion of a job for life is not entirely a thing of the past, many would argue that the nature and shape of career has continued to evolve over recent years. Bimrose, Barnes and Hughes (2008) and Hearne (2010) assert that the modern career is likely to be less predictable and certainly less linear, particularly in times of economic recession. This means that there is a need to develop an ability to negotiate and manage career within this context (Bimrose and Hearne, 2012).

In many contexts the term 'risk' is associated with 'resilience'. Resilience is often developed through adversity, and individuals need to learn how to measure risk and to manage it. The idea of perseverance is important here too, although this is only one element of resilience. Bimrose and Hearne (2012) relate the term 'resilience' to the concept of 'career adaptability'. So resilience is not just the ability to bounce back from adversity, but also being able to adapt approaches, manage risk and develop strategies for success through the experience of it. Rather than continuing to keep trying (like the spider in the story of Robert the Bruce – see the lesson plan in Chapter 6), the resilient person adapts their approach to new situations and new opportunities in the light of feedback. In this process, risk is recognised, measured and embraced as an opportunity, and the need for adaptability is acknowledged.

Rather than the metaphor of the persevering spider, the idea of the copse is helpful in this regard. Imagine a tree with a single trunk which is felled near to its base. To those without an understanding of trees, this would appear to be the end of the story. However, after a period of time, a number of small shoots can be seen emerging from the freshly cut base. Gradually, these grow until, instead of a single, thick, straight trunk, we see a considerable number of smaller, slim branches growing into what looks to the untrained eye to be a bush. What the eye cannot see is that beneath the ground the roots have also subdivided and grown thick and wide. The result – the copse – is a site of burgeoning growth.

So how does this help to explain the importance of career adaptability and resilience? For some, the loss of a linear career (the single trunk of the straight, thick tree) enables a more varied, and arguably more resilient, approach to be developed. Roots go deeper and wider, enabling the individual to withstand more adversity and engage in more risk; if one of the branches is broken, there are many more options available. Thus resilience can be seen as a strong blend of coping with adversity, risk taking and adaptability to change. This illustrates the importance of learning, reflection and the management of risk.

Savickas and Porfeli (2012) identified four dimensions of human capital that help to take this one step further and enable us to consider other characteristics of resilience: concern, control, curiosity and confidence. Helpfully, these are not so different to the characteristics Wolin and Wolin (1993) associated with resilience: initiative, independence, insight, relationship, humour and creativity and morality. For example, the development of independence requires some confidence, insight can be achieved through curiosity and morality requires control in the form of self-control. Furthermore, this also offers some possibilities for teaching the skills needed for the development of career resilience and thereby career adaptability.

Career happiness

The anchorage block on the left-hand side of the CLD Bridge represents career happiness. Career happiness is an important value and, as a philosophy of practice, is far more effective in motivating young people to aspire and achieve than the usual deficit-and-disaster tactics! What are students learning about themselves and the meaning of work if their teachers are constantly haranguing them about not working hard enough and what will happen to them if they don't pass their exams? Career happiness is a foundation stone of an inspiring CLD programme.

At first glance, career happiness can seem to be a fuzzy concept. First, we need to consider what we mean by career happiness. We argue that career is the ongoing narrative of an individual's work experiences and achievements looked at in relation to his or her life as a whole. Work includes the effort individuals put into learning, into personal and voluntary or gift work and into paid jobs or economic work. The benefit of a holistic definition such as this is that it firmly places a person's career in the context of his or her other life roles and domains which permits a much fuller explanation of the person's choices, decisions, plans, actions and outcomes. It also places the pursuit of happiness in the context of his or her life as a whole. The drawback is that it can blur the boundaries between career and life, and thus between careers education and overall education. This can make it more difficult in practice to identify boundaries and focus activities/interventions in the CLD programme.

Keyes, Shmotkin and Ryff (2002) describe happiness as the subjective experience of pleasure and positive feelings of well-being. They identify two interrelated components of psychological well-being that help individuals to flourish: hedonic and eudaemonic well-being.

Hedonic well-being refers to enjoyment of the pleasurable moments in life. While hedonic moments give individuals the most intense feelings of happiness, they are not the norm. The euphoria of finding out that you have succeeded in getting a place on the degree course of your choice is soon succeeded by a realisation that you now have three years of study ahead of you!

Eudaemonic well-being relates to the underpinning, longer-lasting but less intense feelings of happiness that come from things such as the following:

- Being accepting of yourself and others
- Fitting in
- Contributing to your own well-being and the well-being of others

- Having a sense of meaning in your life
- Being in control and realising your personal growth and potential.

Hopefully, during those three years of study at university, students will experience many moments of flow (Csíkszentmihályi, 1990) when they are completely 'lost' in the work they are doing. This kind of happiness is about contentment, harmony and the absence of anxiety or desire. Career happiness, therefore, is related to people's evaluation of the pleasure and well-being they derive from their engagement in learning and work, and it is affected by what is happening to them in other major life domains such as their family, leisure, civic and community lives.

Second, why does career happiness matter? The pursuit of career happiness might seem a luxury when jobs for young people are hard to come by, but it is positively associated with good things in life such as optimism, finding purpose in life, developing positive relationships with others, having a sense of humour, enjoying good health and feeling fulfilled. Many disciplines shed a light on why happiness matters including positive psychology, neuroscience, sociology, economics, political science and philosophy. Gaining happiness at the expense of others, for example, raises moral concerns. Career is a socially-managed concept, and in society, the right to a career carries with it an obligation that people should not choose work that harms others. In other words, they should perform work that contributes to their own well-being (selfishness in the positive sense of the word) and to the well-being of others. So it is not sufficient that behaving in a particular way in their career is fine if it just makes the individual happy.

Similarly, political scientists have argued that the pursuit and enjoyment of happiness is a right that places obligations on governments in democratic systems to create the conditions that will enable people to flourish. This throws the spotlight on careers education and guidance as a public good and the policies that national governments should adopt in support of it.

And third, how can we teach career happiness? Research suggests that young people need to learn seven essential habits of mind if they want to be happy in their careers (see 'Tips for career happiness'). Much, but not all, of the learning related to career happiness is 'caught' not 'taught'. Young people are influenced incidentally and informally by family, friends and the people around them; but this way of learning can be harnessed in the formal curriculum (see Chapter 2). The overarching aims of teaching career happiness are to help young people discover the following:

- What makes them happy
- What career happiness is and what their opportunities for career happiness are
- How to maximise their career happiness.

TIPS FOR CAREER HAPPINESS

1. Learn to understand yourself and express your emotions

Metacognitive understanding and emotional intelligence equip young people to know their own minds and feelings, to be self-determining and to possess self-efficacy beliefs. These agentic qualities enable individuals to recognise and articulate their needs, interests, values, attitudes and beliefs, and to find happiness and well-being. It helps them choose intrinsically motivating work activities that will help them achieve a state of 'flow'.

2. Cultivate a positive and optimistic attitude to work and life

A 'glass half full' attitude and learned optimism are keys to career happiness. Many popular sayings sum this up (e.g. 'every cloud has a silver lining', 'the harder I work the luckier I get'). Young people need to acknowledge their own temperament and recognise the conditions that will help them develop a positive attitude (e.g. imbibing a positive work ethic from others around them, doing things they enjoy and engaging in types of work that are useful and worthwhile). For many people, a positive attitude to work and life is rooted in gratitude and appreciation, meditation, spirituality and religious belief.

3. Contribute to the well-being of others

In their careers, individuals are expected to contribute to their own well-being and the well-being of others in society. The test of universal career happiness is not 'Do you enjoy behaving in this way? Yes. That's OK then', but 'Would the world be a happier place to live in if everyone were to behave in the way you do?' Altruism and kindness to others increases people's baseline happiness.

4. Work on your relationships with others

Social relationships have a strong influence on happiness. Individuals have acceptance and affiliation needs that can be met by working well with others. Being part of a close and supportive team contributes to the happiness and well-being of the self and others.

5. Make the best use of your choices and opportunities

People can be happy even when they have few choices. They can draw on a positive outlook, adaptability and resilience to make the most of their situation whilst acknowledging that they would like their lives to be different. Of course, this situation is far from ideal if they are missing out on choices and opportunities that they do not know about, cannot afford or do not know how to bring about. Individuals can do a lot to help themselves by evaluating job opportunities carefully (e.g. what is the management culture of the organisation they are thinking of joining and what is the managerial style of those they will be working for?). It is the perceived injustices and lack of appreciation that can erode career happiness on a day-to-day basis.

6. Make sense of your achievements and success

Managing your performance or success has a considerable bearing on happiness. Young people can derive great motivation and pleasure from committing to their goals and accomplishing them, rising to challenges and developing new abilities. Achievement can give them the intense highs that happiness can bring, but at the far reaches of success, fame and the need to go on achieving can be difficult to handle. Knowing how to respond to personal success is a key ingredient of staying happy.

7. Be thankful

Striving for career happiness is not so that individuals can be happy all the time. Much has been written and said about the motivating effects of learning from setbacks and disappointment. Nevertheless, rather than trying too hard to be happy, individuals can learn to recognise and appreciate the happiness within them. Being able to receive and express gratitude is a powerful ingredient of this.

Career growth

The road that spans the CLD Bridge represents career growth. Throughout their lives, people will need to traverse the CLD Bridge in both directions (from education to the world of work and back again via lifelong learning) as they seek to respond to changes in their circumstances, the fluctuating economy and the range of uncertainties in their lives more generally. There are two aspects of career growth as follows.

The career narrative

Recent thinking on career development focuses on career as something that is constructed throughout life. In the past, it was argued that a good career decision was a rational, logical one that could be justified. However, much research shows that this is not necessarily how people make their career decisions. Other factors often come into play, whether it is our emotional response, the limitations of our context or simply being in the right place at the right time. Constructivist approaches to career argue that people actively construct their understanding of career through their own thinking and action. We make sense of the abstract notion of career by telling our story based on our thoughts and experiences so far. This process of thought and action about the past enables us to think about the future and the possibilities that could be open to us. Bruner (1996:35) argues that by talking about our experiences ('self with history') we begin to think about the future ('self with possibility'). CLD, therefore, needs to provide opportunities for young people to engage in a range of activities where they can tell their story; by doing so, they can begin to see their future possibilities more clearly.

The zone of proximal development (ZPD)

Previously in this chapter, we proposed that knowledge about career is constructed through participation in activity and in interactions with others. The concept of the ZPD is helpful in explaining how people learn. Wood (1998:26) defines the ZPD as 'the gap that exists for an individual child (or adult) between what he is able to do alone, and what he (sic) can achieve with help from one more knowledgeable than himself'. However, it is important to understand that from this perspective, learning does not happen by the learner being shown what to do by the more experienced person in a didactic way. Here, learning is active and practical, where the more experienced person helps learners to develop by prompting them with questions and offering alternatives to enable them to learn for themselves. This means that learning about career in the ZPD is as follows:

- Practical
- Participative
- A social process
- Always culturally situated
- Done in partnership and dialogue with a more experienced person/people
- Focused on problem solving.

Two particular aspects of learning in the ZPD are worthy of note.

- Over time, help and support from the more experienced person needs to be reduced as the learner gains new knowledge and develops the required skills.
- The overall aim is that the learner grows in independence. What the learner can do with help today, he or she will be able to do alone in the future.

'Proximal' is not a word that we use often in everyday language, but it means nearness and closeness to the point of attachment or observation. We often learn in a step-by-step way, from the foundations of a subject moving forward to more complex concepts. For example, most of us would struggle with A-level Physics if we had not studied it at the GCSE level. Learning about career in the ZPD is similar in this respect; it means focusing on what the young person can learn next. This is not only in relation to time (what do I do next, e.g. at the end of compulsory schooling), but also in relation to self (what do I need to learn about myself next, e.g. how I view my skills, abilities, attitudes and values) and in relation to decision making (e.g. what are my options at this point?). Thinking about career often involves thinking strategically – how can I put myself in the best possible position to achieve what I hope to achieve? This will mean thinking about the next steps in relation to a number of different options and evaluating them side by side.

CLD can give young people the opportunity to learn more with the help and support of others than they can alone, and the ultimate goal of CLD is that young people will develop into mature, independent adults who can think about their career in an ongoing way. What they learn in CLD at school they will then be able to practise throughout their lives.

The metaphor of growth is helpful in a number of ways in relation to CLD. It is worth bearing in mind that plants grow and flourish if the following conditions occur:

- They are fed and watered.
- They have enough sunlight.
- They are pruned.
- They are in fertile ground.

The same applies to young people and their career growth.

However, it is also important to understand that career growth does not always appear to happen in a sequential way. For example, students may have had an idea about their future for some time, but through the process of telling their story and looking at the next steps,

Table 1.2 What is needed for growth to occur

Plants	*Young people*
Need to be fed and watered	Need activities and experience to help them to learn about careers
Need enough sunlight	Need support and encouragement and can learn more with others than they can alone
Need to be pruned	Will experience difficult situations (e.g. rejections), but these will help to build their resilience
Need fertile ground	Need a positive learning environment where they can take risks without fear of failure and receive constructive feedback

they may then begin to change their minds. This can feel like going backwards ('I thought I knew what I wanted to do, but now I don't'). However, this is still an important part of the process of career growth, where some students need to go backwards in order to gain greater clarity to then be able to move forward. It is worth remembering that after pruning a plant (such as a vine), it can often appear from the outside as if it might not survive, when in fact growth is often happening beneath the surface. This can also be the case with young people, especially if they have experienced something that has had a negative impact on their confidence.

Conclusion

In Chapters 4, 5 and 6, we develop the concepts of career resilience, career happiness and career growth further and give examples of the skills which can be developed and nurtured within CLD, thereby enabling young people to develop. This guide will show you how to deliver CLD effectively to enable young people to develop the knowledge and skills they need to establish a balance between career resilience and career happiness, and to maintain career growth throughout their lives. In the next chapter, we move on to examine how CLD can be taught.

Chapter 2

Teaching for CLD

Introduction

In Chapter 1, we used the metaphor of the CLD Bridge to express the overarching purpose of careers teaching. Promoting career resilience, happiness and growth belongs at the heart of everyday practice. In this chapter, we identify teaching approaches that empower learners directly to take control of their own CLD.

Supporting effective career guidance

If career guidance was just about passing on information, then teaching that facilitated information recall would be sufficient to prepare students for their careers interviews. Similarly, if the only purpose of career guidance was to prepare students to make decisions and plans based on the results of 'objective' career assessments, then teaching that strengthened rational thought processes would be enough. Career guidance is much more sophisticated, and careers teaching needs to be too:

- Many careers advisers use constructivist theory and techniques (Savickas, 2005) to help individuals make sense of their experiences, to create positive patterns and to act confidently in their lives. Careers teaching needs to strengthen young people's independence as learners. It needs to provide rich career learning experiences, especially those that facilitate cooperative learning. It needs to foster mindfulness and thinking about their own thinking so that they can use reflection and abductive reasoning (inference) to tell versions of their past, present and future stories.
- Some careers advisers use insights from the chaos theory of careers (Pryor and Bright, 2011) to help individuals deal with career complexity, change and unpredictability (e.g. by examining case studies). Careers teaching needs to strengthen young people's ability to be creative, solve problems, embrace change and apply learning in new situations.

This means we are looking at ways of enabling individuals to do the following:

- Become more aware of what is happening to them and in the world about them. Well-targeted teaching interventions can help learners to notice and make sense of their mind and body states and changes that are taking place around them (e.g. when they have 'flow' experiences).
- Flourish within networks of support that they have built around themselves.

- Take action and to keep going or to change direction if that is what is needed to prosper and achieve personal and career well-being.
- Review and reflect on their own thoughts and feelings, on their progress and on the relationships and the responses of others to them.

To do this well, the following needs to occur:

- The environment in which the learning takes place needs to be carefully managed.
- Career practitioners need to demonstrate supporting characteristics.
- Teaching approaches need to be fit for the purpose.

The interplay of these factors affects the quality of the careers teaching experienced by students.

Creating a positive environment for learning

When considering how a positive learning environment can be created, establishing a climate of trust and support is particularly important. Teachers are aware that career learning can involve disclosure and discussion by students of sensitive personal issues. At the outset, those leading sessions should help the students to agree on 'ground rules' about how they want to treat each other. These rules should be put on permanent display. It is the responsibility of staff and students to provide a safe space where there is trust and confidentiality for young people to share their thoughts and feelings; although individuals should also have the right to 'pass'. Sometimes it is more effective to allow individuals to feed in comments anonymously so that they feel safe when raising issues, and the whole group can benefit from the discussion that ensues. These ground rules need to be extended to cover online interactions (e.g. class blogs). Students can also benefit considerably from working in settings that are fit for purpose (e.g. a drama studio or science lab may be ideal in some circumstances but not in others). They also need suitable blocks of time so that they do not feel rushed and can really concentrate and immerse themselves in what they are doing.

Rowe, Wilkin and Wilson's (2012) useful model for effective teaching focuses on the following three key areas:

1. A good teaching environment – is calm, well disciplined, safe and secure; has a positive atmosphere; is purposeful, stimulating and well organised and is delivered in good accommodation with bright displays.
2. Effective teaching approaches – are interactive (social constructivist), with lots of teacher/student dialogue and monitoring of student progress; are concerned with the assessment of students for learning, committed to student agency and voice and well planned and organised; scaffold learning and build on prior knowledge and experience; are personalised, linked with learning at home, in touch with new technology and collaborative (including working closely with teaching assistants) and use external resources (e.g. speakers and visits) creatively.
3. Effective teachers – have good subject knowledge, high levels of self-efficacy belief and high expectations; are motivational; provide challenge; are calm, caring, sensitive and ready to give praise; use humour as a learning and engagement tool; foster trust and mutual respect and are flexible (where appropriate) and reflective.

In relation to issues of equality, it is important in CLD to foster an ethos of aspiration and achievement for all. Whatever the academic ability of individuals, their social or economic grouping or their ethnic or cultural background, CLD should enable individuals to aspire to whatever lies within their potential and whatever interests and excites them and enables them to progress. Hodkinson, Sparkes and Hodkinson (1996) use the phrase 'horizons for action' to describe how the young people in their study made their career decisions. These horizons are formed by notions that the young people had about themselves combined with knowledge of the opportunities around them and their perceptions from their life histories regarding what they felt they could achieve. It is vital that CLD helps young people to expand their horizons for action and thereby achieve their full potential.

The first verse of the poem 'The Road Not Taken' by Robert Frost illustrates this point well. In the poem, the roads diverge, so a decision is required. The traveller is sorry that he cannot take both routes. He looks as far as he can see, but to see more, he will have to move forward to extend his horizon. This poem can be used in CLD to help students to think about the choices they will have to make and how they can extend their horizons for action.

Characteristics of effective career practitioners

Students respond well to careers staff who have their best interests at heart and with whom they feel a rapport. Staff can improve career learning for students by doing the following:

- Being well prepared and well organized.
- Being consistent and fair.
- Setting realistically high aspirations and challenges, e.g. by outlining clear learning goals, making the learning relevant and building in the right amount of challenge (this is important in relation to learning in the ZPD and engendering states of flow).
- Modelling the skills associated with career resilience, happiness and growth so that students 'catch' the outcomes that staff are seeking for them.
- Using humour to engage students in their own CLD.
- Using coaching techniques (affirmation, visualisation, distraction, etc.) with students to motivate them, focus their minds, set goals and enable them to feel more positive about themselves. (Turnbull, 2009)

Teaching approaches

Students can benefit from a wide range of teaching approaches, but the pedagogies that support independent, reflective, participative and experiential learning are among the most effective in promoting career resilience, happiness and growth. For each of the approaches we describe subsequently, we identify the following:

- What it is
- Why use it
- How to use it well.

Portfolio learning

What it is

A portfolio is a rich environment for learners to tell their own stories, cultivate optimism, record their experiences and manage their own plans. In essence, it is a collection created by a student to show their progress and achievements. An artist's portfolio, for example, will contain a range of pieces that could stand on their own but together say more about the artist. More broadly, it is also a self-portrait, presenting not only information about the individual but also their ideas, perspectives and interpretations of that information.

The whole is greater than the sum of its parts. A portfolio is particularly useful for the following:

- Creating a personal career narrative
- Logging experiences, forming a track record of achievements
- Storing and recording data that students will need to create curricula vitae (CVs), or résumés, and complete applications
- Structuring reflection (e.g. What have I got to be thankful for?).

Why use it

Individuals can use their portfolio to feel more positive about themselves and to feel valued. They can use it to identify what good work looks like and to feel more involved and supported in target-setting and action-planning.

Portfolio learning combines well with other approaches, particularly narrative-based and action-planning approaches. It can also be used in traditional ways to collect and assess the work they have been doing in careers and other subjects of the curriculum. Evidence from their portfolios can also be extracted to support applications they are making. It can become the organising environment for the whole of the careers programme.

A careers portfolio can also be integrated with the school's student information, tracking and assessment system, providing the school recognises that their purposes are different. It can also be used for 'conferencing' or progress reviews where individuals discuss the content of their portfolio with their tutors, parents and teachers.

How to use it well

When considering the use of portfolios, it is worth remembering that students will want to:

- Use their portfolios differently, so it is important to reassure them that this is alright. Be prepared to answer the following questions:
    - What's in it for me?
    - How do I do it right?
    - What do you think so far? (This question will be asked by the person who just loves writing their life story and is on a second ring binder already!)
- Know which parts of the portfolio can be for their own private use and which parts are 'owned' jointly with the school.
- Personalise the look and feel of their portfolios.

- Make use of digital technologies for ease of use, storage and sharing parts of the portfolio with others (free and commercial e-portfolio systems are available). It is important to show students how to safeguard themselves and choose privacy settings if they use social media for building a portfolio. There are many stories of selectors discovering unfortunate information about applicants online.
- Enjoy developing their portfolios, so it is important to vary the portfolio-building activities so that learners do not become bored.

The plan-do-review cycle is well-suited to the portfolio approach (see the subsequent box). Tutors and mentors can support learners by helping them to put together their action plans, carry them out and review their progress/achievement. This will trigger learners' use of their portfolios at key decision and transition points such as choosing their post-16 education (P16) options.

THE PLAN-DO-REVIEW CYCLE

The basic cycle is as follows:

Plan – Where am I now? Where do I want to be? How will I get there?
Do – Carry out the plan. Access own network of support.
Review – How did it go? What will I do differently or better next time? What will I do next?

The evidence that this approach is effective comes from studies of self-efficacy (when individuals believe in their ability to get things done) and goal-setting behaviour (people who give themselves goals and work out a specific plan for getting there achieve more than those who are more vague and unfocused).

The subsequent box suggests ways of using portfolios in CLD for young people.

WAYS OF USING PORTFOLIOS

- Writing narratives. My story so far, my story with optional endings and the middle-aged me narrative can be very powerful. Students could start with a simple timeline with key events, transitions and achievements identified and then elaborate chosen sections of the story, exploring feelings about choice and change, risk and adventure. Savickas and Hartung (2012) describe career as a story within which there are chapters. Indecision over the next step to take is the equivalent of 'writer's block', and you could play the role of the writer's coach. The only way to see how the next chapter will reveal itself is to revisit the previous ones and to write alternative endings to their stories (e.g. if I go to college and study for a Business Degree, if I travel for a while, if I take a job and live with my cousin in the city . . .).

Encourage students to include photographs, testimonies, cuttings, artwork or let-ters and reports to help them to see themselves in the story. The accuracy of the story in reality is irrelevant, only that they can see possibilities and themselves from a new angle. The elements of the story are important, and you could help your students by suggesting that they include specific words or phrases in their stories such as excitement, events, dilemma, problem, disagreement, unfortunately, finally, luckily, so, surpris-ingly and so on. You could also use a visual tool to help students with writing their stories, such as the Story Mountain (Communication 4 All, n.d.).

Be prepared to share your own story when asked questions such as the following:

> So what's your story?
> How did you get to do this job?
> What would you like to do next?

- Many activities are available to help individuals to list or consider their strengths and abilities. They range from the simple list of 'what I'm good at' and 'my qualities' to the products of complex psychometric testing. What is perhaps more important than the list itself (as this will certainly change over time) is the reflec-tive skill that is needed to identify them. 'What I'm good at' may not be the same as 'what others say I'm good at'. If the student excels in a wide range of areas, then what he or she perceives to be average ability may be judged by another as outstanding. In other words, these judgements are subjective, influenced by the significant others around and by the embedded discourse such as 'Alex has always been sporty' even if in fact Alex is also a very able artist.

It can also be helpful for students to ask peers to share their insights. Questions such as the following can help students gain the perspectives of others and add to their growing self-awareness:

> What three words would you use to describe me?
> What do you think I am really good at?
> If you were me, what would you work on?

- Students can use their portfolios to develop their knowledge and understand-ing of their options at each transition point (e.g. researching the availability and accessibility of different options and the prospects they open up). Students can present their findings in creative ways (e.g. through posters, presentations, col-lages, poetry, drama or songs).
- Students can also use their portfolios to clarify their long-term goals, dreams and ideals – the fundamental element/s of possible career directions that are non-negotiable such as social equity, creativity, financial reward, sustainability and political change. Ask the students to ask themselves 'what are the most important values in my life that drive my career decisions?' Ask your students to draw or make a collage of their idea of the perfect world of work. They might select pic-tures showing such things as team work, exploration, achievement and personal fulfilment. This is not the same as asking them to picture their ideal future or dream because that is likely to elicit simplistic concepts of wealth or fame. How-ever, there is some useful learning to come from dreaming.

The 'Dream Cloud' activity in Unit 2 of *The Real Game* (Prospects, 2005) encourages dreaming, of possessions, houses, lifestyles and image, and uses the safe space of a game to check the realism of those dreams and the choices that would have to be made to achieve them. The crucial aspect of this part of the game is that the Dream Cloud is always left on display – or in the portfolio. The dream is never over.

- What we believe about ourselves is important, but unexamined self-beliefs can leave some young people struggling to make good decisions and achieve satisfactory relationships. Self-confidence is crucial for resilience as we have already discussed in Chapter 1. However, if the qualities we believe we have are not shared by others, we need to review things. A portfolio can be a safe way of exploring parents', teachers' and friends' perceptions of us using a technique such as the Johari window (Luft and Ingham, 1955).
- A portfolio should contain evidence that the individual is aware of, and has accessed, the help and support available. Asking for help requires trust, recognition of need, making an effort and the skills to assess the quality, professionalism and impartiality of the helper. Careers advisers need to be aware of the sensitivity in some cultures about asking for help.

Tests and questionnaires

What they are

There are a variety of tests and questionnaires on the market to help students to explore their interests and abilities, which then match the person to a range of possible career options. Whilst some would argue that the matching model is now dated, the number of tests and questionnaires available is testament to its endurance. Whilst some are costed, there are also a number of free packages available.

Why use them

One of the many reasons that young people find learning about career difficult is that most find the concept of career abstract. Any method that helps to make things more concrete for them is to be welcomed. Here tests and questionnaires can help. They can act as idea generators for those students who feel they do not have any firm ideas about the future. For those who do have career ideas, a test or questionnaire can help to reassure them by confirming their thoughts and can also make suggestions of similar career areas to help them to broaden their ideas.

How to use them well

Tests and questionnaires can be very helpful tools but always need to be used in a timely way with students for whom they are appropriate. It is doubtful that all students will be ready for them at the same time, so the use of them in a blanket way (e.g. with a particular year group) will only be helpful for some. Such methods should also only be used when there is time for feedback and discussion so that students can then interpret their results with some help and support. This means that those administering tests and questionnaires need to be knowledgeable about the scope of the particular test being used (what it can and cannot do) and the format of the results.

~y-based learning

~ is

~ methods involve young people in finding answers to the questions that are important ~, for example:

ould I choose an apprenticeship over higher education (HE)?
n money buy happiness?
~at should I do if they don't treat me well on work experience?

~ples of useful enquiry-based methods include the following:

~uctured question and answer discussions, e.g. inviting back former students to talk ~ut what to look out for when choosing HE.
~alogic teaching, e.g. using structured talk to extend students' thinking.
~jects, investigations and fieldwork, e.g. researching a topic such as 'the experience of ~men graduates in the architectural profession' or testing a hypothesis such as 'the best ~ployers focus their recruitment activities on students at Russell Group universities'.
~blem-based learning, e.g. students investigate strategies for securing a positional ~antage when applying for places on highly sought after degree courses.

~e it

~ methods that capture knowledge, stimulate thinking and develop ideas are well ~o learners who are theorists and reflectors in Honey and Mumford's (2000) model ~ing styles. Learning about career resilience, happiness and growth in this way ~t readily translate into visible outcomes in these areas; to change their behav- ~arners have to be able to internalise the learning and make it transferable to new ~ns. Problem-based learning facilitates this more than teacher-led exposition and ~n-and-answer sessions. Learners described by Honey and Mumford as pragmatists ~ivists prefer to experience things first and then consider the information and ideas ~se from what they have done. Experiential activities (see the next section) can ~ung people to become more receptive to the discussion of big ideas. In this way, ~ put together learning sequences that combine different learning approaches for ~m effect.

use it well

~ns for investigation can be devised by teachers, but they can also emerge from the ~e between students and teachers. Projects and investigations that give students ~ny and choice are more engaging, so students can be encouraged to create questions ~own. 'Happiness economics', for example, provides a rich source of issues around ~tudents can frame investigations such as the following:

~o measures happiness most accurately: economists, philosophers, psychologists or ~iologists?
~es money make people happy?

It is also worth considering the downsides of using these n
caution come to mind. There is great danger in using these m
niques. All students will need help and support with interpretin
about what they need to do next. In some situations, there i
questionnaire might raise completely different ideas to the on
any given time. In such cases, students will need help and suppc
be the case. Any students who are left with test results to fath
be discouraged and even make grave mistakes (see the case stu

PETER

Peter was an able student with wide-ranging interests in Art
Maths (and subsequently Economics) and English, so he fc
thinking about career very difficult as potentially he had so r
was in Year 10, when it seemed to him that many of his frien
wanted to do, all the students in his year completed a set of
generated a number of career ideas for research and consid
time, Peter was very interested in fashion, as demonstrated
particularly trainers.

Having completed the psychometric tests, Peter receiv
later, and several career areas were suggested, ranked in or
and suitability. Peter was given no support in interpreting t
he quickly skipped towards the end of the list to the sug
Peter became very interested in this, fuelled by his love of
he attended a fashion summer school at a college. Follow
A levels in art, maths and economics, he went to art coll
course for fashion. As soon as he started college, he felt tha
the students had strong practical skills in sewing, which he d
the atmosphere. Peter left after the first term and decided
something different. He also travelled around Europe.

When Peter reached the final year of his undergraduate
he began to think about his skills and talents. He had been
newspaper, editing the fashion section (which he loved), sc
journalism. Through this work, he also came across the idea
to do some research into this area too. After some very ca
the two areas (e.g. what the work itself involved, training n
Peter went on to a professional course in advertising.

Peter now works in advertising where, as a strategic pla
research into consumer markets (economics), design Pow
'pitches' to clients (art), write narratives and scripts for TV
engage in discussion about the 'big ideas' that increase sales (
back at the results of the tests he did in Year 10, the first ide
was advertising, with journalism and publishing coming a cl
possible that a closer exploration of these results at the time m
time and the costly mistake of going to art college – but of c

---

Enqu

What

Enqui
to the

- S
- C
- V

Ex

- S
  al
- D
- P
  w
  e
- P
  ac

Why

Enqui
suited
of lea
does i
iour, l
situati
questi
and ac
that a
help y
you ca
maxin

How t

Quest
dialog
auton
of the
which

- W
  sc
- D

- Does having a job make people happy?
- Does having children increase or decrease happiness?
- Do leisure pursuits increase happiness?

Rigour in enquiry-based learning comes from the methods used to gather, analyse and interpret the evidence collected. The teacher can decide how much guidance and structure students need to carry out an enquiry.

Interactive learning

What it is

Digital technology has made possible new ways for young people to interact with each other and the world by, for example:

- Staying connected and communicating through social media
- Sharing information using well-designed apps and software
- Accessing virtual worlds for gaming and other learning and leisure purposes.

Mobile devices are becoming ever more powerful and versatile, while 'gesture-based computing' and 'the Internet of things' are opening up new opportunities for organising career learning.

Interactive learning approaches encourage the following:

- Peer-to-peer based learning or paragogy (Corneli and Danoff, 2011), e.g. students generating their own content and learning from each other and especially from individuals with whom they feel an affinity.
- Connectivism (Siemens, 2004), e.g. students knowing how to find knowledge, exploit networks and learn collaboratively with others (including the possibilities of co-learning with teachers).
- Self-determined learning or heutagogy (Hase and Kenyon, 2000), e.g. students regulating their own learning, improving their own learning skills as they learn and learning in both formal and informal settings.

Why use it

The benefits for students of using interactive learning approaches for CLD are as follows:

- Fast and easy access to information. Students do not have to wait for a careers lesson or go to a library; they can simply scan a quick response (QR) code, enter a search term in their browser, download an app or watch a video clip on their tablet or smartphone.
- A wide choice of ways of creating, sharing and presenting information. Students can send tweets and create individual or class blogs, wikis, forums and podcasts to share useful knowledge. They can use standard office tools and authoring and editing software to create e-learning content.

The following are benefits for schools:

- Learning is no longer tied to the classroom or timetabled careers lessons. Learning can be 'flipped' so that students start off learning outside the classroom (e.g. watch a video or carry out a WebQuest), and when the lesson takes place, the teacher can interact with the students in more interesting ways.
- Students can help themselves, help each other and take pressure off careers staff.

How to use it well

Interactive learning presents a number of challenges:

- Students need help to evaluate online sources of information and to avoid being swamped by the sheer amount of information on the Web. One way of helping students to overcome this is to create a virtual careers library or centre on the school's virtual learning environment (VLE) or learning platform and to select only the best career learning and information sites to go on it. You will need to schedule time for the design, maintenance and updating of your online pages, portals and platforms, but remember that students can engage with this process too.
- The new technology does not drive out the old, i.e. interactive learning is not an alternative to face-to-face learning but an enhancement.
- Don't be afraid to step outside your comfort zone if information and communication technology (ICT) is not your thing – your students will show you the way! It is also a good idea to talk to your school's ICT managers and technicians, find out what digital technology your school is using and what its capabilities are and ask for their help in using it in your careers work.
- Choose media and tools that are inspiring and motivating to use. Question your assumption that students can only learn if you teach it to them. They should only need to think about the technology they're using about 1% of the time!

The subsequent box suggests ways of harnessing digital technology for interactive learning.

IDEAS FOR HARNESSING DIGITAL TECHNOLOGY

- Encourage students to create a personal careers portfolio using readily available blog software (such as http://www.blogger.com/, http://www.flickr.com, http://www.tumblr.com/, http://www.wallwisher.com and http://www.wordpress.com). Investigate other interesting ways of creating portfolios, e.g. mind maps (such as http://vue.tufts.edu and http://www.mapmyself.com) and pinboards (http://pinterest.com).
- Facilitate student-generated content such as the following:
  - o   Podcasts
  - o   School radio

o   Wikis

o   Class blogs (Start a 'Question Chain' in a class blog – the first student posts a question, e.g. 'Why do men earn more than women?' A second student answers it and poses a new question, and so on.)

o   Polls and surveys (such as http://www.surveymonkey.com/).

• Highlight cutting edge practices to your students, such as the following:

o   Mentoring (http://www.horsesmouth.co.uk)

o   Employment agencies that enable companies to hire online freelancers (such as https://www.elance.com/ and https://www.odesk.com/)

o   Using QR codes to access information

o   Careers apps.

• Create your own careers blog and encourage students to comment on your posts so that all students can benefit from the discussions that take place.

• Start tweeting to pass on nuggets of information and advice to your students that they will retweet to their friends.

• Develop the careers pages on your school or college website and/or VLE for students and parents/carers to use 24/7.

• Create a dashboard to organise and display your careers resources. Netvibes is an example of dashboard software (http://about.netvibes.com/).

• Arrange resources on the dashboard in a sequence to take students on a learning journey. The sequence for intending HE students, for example, could be as follows:

01   Choosing HE

02   Taking a gap year

03   Studying abroad

04   Applying to HE

05   Where and what to study

06   Student finance

07   Student housing

08   Student life

09   Graduate and postgraduate study.

• Create e-learning resources using presentation software (e.g. PowerPoint and Prezi) or, for more advanced practitioners, using authoring software (e.g. Articulate Presenter, Articulate Storyline or Adobe Captivate).

• Use an online environment such as Second Life to enable students to attend careers fairs and lessons and interact with each other (e.g. working collaboratively on a careers project). Organise a mixed-reality classroom so that students from other schools can participate in your careers lesson via Second Life. Set up webinars to organise similar activities.

Active learning

What it is

'Active learning' is an umbrella term for a group of teaching methods that share some or all of the following characteristics:

- Learning by doing
- Group exercises (see also 'cooperative learning')
- Real or authentic contexts
- Dynamic skill development (e.g. leadership, decision making and problem solving by students themselves).

Examples related to careers and the world of work include the following:

- In-tray and e-tray exercises
- Design-and-make simulations
- Production simulations
- Problem-based case studies
- Business games, role plays and simulations.

Why use it

Active learning is based on social constructivist principles, e.g. personal autonomy and engagement, collaboration and reflection. It supports self-regulation, reciprocal teaching and holistic learning, e.g. activities focused on relevant real-life situations and problems that give students opportunities to develop and apply knowledge and skills that they can learn from the teacher and each other.

How to use it well

You will be able to find a wide range of published careers and work-related active learning exercises to suit your purposes, but it is more fun to be creative and adventurous in writing your own exercises. These are the main steps in getting started:

- Identify a main idea or key issue, e.g. critical path analysis used in project management.
- Choose a situation that exemplifies it, e.g. building a quiet garden and wooden shelter in the school grounds.
- Involve someone from outside the school who has relevant expertise and can help design the activity, advise students and judge their plans, e.g. an operational researcher, a landscape architect or a project manager.
- Add a problem or difficulty, e.g. after the students have drawn up their critical path, they are notified that the mayor is coming a week earlier than planned to open the garden.
- Decide on the most appropriate format (role play, case study, game, etc.), e.g. it could be run as a case study.

To get the most out of an active learning exercise, it is also important to do the following:

- Make sure you have all the materials and resources you need at hand
- Work out appropriate timings

- Debrief students straight away
- Evaluate the impact of the activity on students' learning.

Cooperative learning

What it is

Cooperative learning involves students learning interdependently in groups or teams to achieve a shared goal. It is more than just students working individually while sitting around the same big table. This definition tells us the following:

- Students must collaborate to enhance the learning process and the outcomes for each member of the group.
- The size and composition of the group can be varied, but this needs to be managed to ensure that the group has the right combination of skills and resources to complete the task.
- Students need to clarify the goal they are working towards and structure the way they work in order to achieve their purpose. Where goals are ambiguous or absent, individuals may follow their own agendas at the expense of the group. Over its lifetime, the social interactions and productivity of the group will vary.

Why use it

Structured cooperative learning activities have an important contribution to make to students' CLD. Cooperative learning supports creativity, active participation, individual responsibility and higher level learning. It helps to meet young people's affiliation needs and, therefore, contributes to their career resilience, happiness and growth.

Cooperative learning is good preparation for the world of work. It helps students understand day-to-day learning in the workplace and how teams can be creative and successful. Vitally, it gives insights into how to tackle workplace segregation and stereotyping. The social dynamics of cooperative learning in the classroom mirror the conditions of the workplace. Much of the work done by people in industry involves interdependence between work teams, departments and even whole companies to generate products and services. The teacher can simulate these conditions by organising everything from simple thinking activities (e.g. brainstorming, think-pair-share and jigsaws) to business simulations and challenges where groups develop products or services in competition with each other. Students often express a preference for working with their friends, but they should experience working with people who are not initially their friends as this is more typical of working conditions.

How to use it well

Cooperative learning processes need to be managed by the teacher and the participants themselves. Students do not automatically enjoy splitting learning tasks between themselves, and they are not always productive and successful which is why students need to be given plenty of practice to develop their skills of learning and working in this way. Groups need time, for example, to learn how to achieve their goals while at the same time to look after their members. As students build up their social capital and sense of responsibility to others, problems such as individuals not pulling their weight, free-riding and 'group think' tend to diminish.

Careful monitoring of tasks, roles and relationships helps to improve the performance of groups, but the teacher needs to make sure that students do not lapse into a pattern where members always take the same roles and thus limit their experience and learning. Cooperation improves where students know about how to optimise each of the stages in the life cycle of a group (described by Tuckman and Jensen, 1977, as forming, storming, norming, performing and adjourning – sometimes called mourning). Keeping a feelings log will help the group to record their successes and setbacks, what went well and what they would do the same or differently next time they are learning cooperatively.

Peer-to-peer–based teaching is a powerful cooperative learning tool. Young people like to take their cue from other young people that they can identify with and so adopt their approach to investigating choices and making plans. Creating a culture in which student role models can influence what other students do is worth trying. Similarly, training a team of careers champions to inform and support other groups of students can be a very effective way of mobilising resources for career learning.

Experiential learning

What it is

In CLD, the environment for learning is not always the classroom. Learning in the wider world, perhaps within a working context or an extra-curricular setting can be appropriate and offer an enhancement to individuals' learning, whilst broadening their understanding of themselves in a different context. Learning from direct experience is a powerful way to learn, and by this we mean instances where students can participate in the labour market (e.g. through work experience, a part-time job or enterprise activities) rather than in experiences that are simulated. Such experiences can be few and far between because of the demands of the curriculum, health, safety and insurance issues for employers and the time needed to organise large-scale activities. However, when given such opportunities, the benefits for students can be enormous as they offer the chance to participate actively in the real world of work.

Why use it

It is fair to say that nothing beats the actual experience of work when it comes to helping students to learn about career. Anything that gives students an opportunity to experience the world of work for themselves is to be welcomed. However, asking them to 'jump in at the deep end' and 'swim' can be very unhelpful and erode their confidence.

How to use it well

In order to benefit from experiential learning, students will need more than just the experience itself. Sessions, or discussions, that help them to progress around Kolb's (1984) learning cycle will be particularly beneficial. Following any experience, students need to be given the opportunity to reflect on what they have learned from it, to see how it helps them to build on the knowledge they already have in order to prepare them for the next experience.

As well as helping students to learn more about the world of work, and perhaps even the area of work they would like or not like to go into, such experiences help students to learn more about themselves. Keeping a reflective diary during a period of work experience, for example, can help them to think at a deeper level, in order to realise more of what they have been learning. To do this effectively, students can be asked to consider the following questions:

- What experience did I gain today, this week?
- How did I feel?
- What assumptions did I make about work?
- Were these correct?
- What have I learned about working life?
- How will this help me in my CLD?
- What do I feel I need to learn next?

Students also need opportunities to reflect on their experiences through discussion, for example with their peers, teachers, other adults and employers too. It is worth remembering that without such opportunities, learning can be severely limited and even forgotten.

Assessing CLD

The main role of assessment in CLD is to check the outcomes of previous learning and to take these results into account when designing the next phase of the learning process so that the student can continue to make progress in achieving career resilience, happiness and growth. This approach is known as 'assessment for learning' in contrast to 'assessment of learning'. Assessment of career learning and indeed accreditation are not necessarily inappropriate, but care must be taken to ensure that they are not misused:

- It would be wholly wrong to suggest on the basis of marked work or an exam that an individual was a personal failure.
- An assessment activity that conformed to one teacher's view of what constituted successful career management might be simplistic at best and mistaken at worst.
- The value of assessment is undermined when the timing is not right for the individual and there is no follow-up provision for helping students to improve.
- Conferring success on learners does, however, have a positive impact on young people's perceptions of themselves, and it is this 'recognition' effect that some schools and special schools in particular try to harness. They celebrate learning success by awarding certificates, holding presentation assemblies (to which they invite parents/carers) and giving rewards (e.g. stickers, House points or reward scheme points).

Studies point to the high level of effectiveness of assessment for learning techniques (Black and William, 1998). Effective assessment for learning involves the following:

- Sharing learning outcomes and performance measures with learners, e.g. by making them explicit at the beginning of the lesson, checking that students understand them and getting feedback from students at the end of the lesson about the progress the students feel they have made.

- Helping learners understand the standards to aim for, e.g. by modelling what is involved in achieving the task. Making sure that learners can recognise what a 'performance of quality' looks like (e.g. by showing examples of exemplary CVs and personal statements).
- Providing feedback that helps learners to identify how to improve their work, e.g. by providing spoken or written comments that tell students what to do next rather than simply giving them a grade or score. Another technique is to use 'feedforward', i.e. to hold a dialogue about what students might do to improve their work before they do it.
- Making the assessment process and the recording of it as straightforward as possible.
- Making the assessment process fun where possible, e.g. by using quizzes, question-naires, sentence completion, line-ups, 'two stars and a wish', hot seat questioning, 'fish bowls', an appointed class rapporteur and 'thumbs up, thumbs down'.
- Self-assessment by learners that can help them to develop as independent learners and to learn how to assess the performance of a team.
- In plenaries, use open questions to elicit deep learning (e.g. 'What were you expected to do?', 'What went well?', 'What would you do differently or better next time?', 'What do you need to do next?' and 'What help do you need?').

Pastoral and learning support

In the final part of this chapter, we examine the support that many young people will need in the CLD process. Many people agree that young people's experiences of the transition from education to work are now much longer than they used to be. Supporting young people through these prolonged transitions can itself be a lengthy process, and in this regard, the concept of the ZPD is again useful. At the Conservative Party conference in 1981, Norman Tebbit, the then Employment Secretary, famously told unemployed people to get 'on your bike' and find work, even if it meant moving to a different part of the country. He was criticized heavily for this subsequently. In this section, the metaphor of helping someone learn how to ride a bike is used as a marked contrast to Tebbit's approach.

Learning how to ride a bike is something that many young children will need help with, and, with some support, most will learn quickly to ride on their own. Indeed, the goal of learning to ride a bike is to be able to ride it independently. Toddlers often begin riding on a tricycle with big, wide wheels as these are easy and fun to ride. As time progresses, they move on to a bicycle with narrow wheels, often with stabilizers for support. In their desire to ride a bike like adults do, one stabilizer is removed to start with, followed by the other. The transition phase of learning how to ride a bike is now well and truly underway.

In many local parks, you can see adults helping their children learn how to ride. First, the adult holds the handlebars and runs alongside; then the adult holds onto the back of the saddle; then the adult begins to let go and finally the child rides independently. Most of this process happens on grass, in order to protect the child from the bumps and grazes that are, inevitably, involved in falling off. Only when the child is confident does he or she begin to ride along paths and, much later, on roads. It is also clear that reading a book about riding a bike or talking to people who can already ride are both good things to do, but they will in no way mean that an individual can then actually ride. Put simply, the only way to learn is by doing.

There is no doubt that young people need support in order to manage their prolonged transitions. The ZPD and the metaphor of learning to ride a bike are useful in the following ways:

- The concept of the ZPD shows that support and guidance need to be proximal to the lives of young people. We need to focus on what young people understand and can do already and then target support to enable them to move to what they can understand and do next. This will, obviously, vary greatly from one young person to another and will involve helping young people to assess their current position and think through the next steps in their development. All of this must be done as part of a gradual move towards independence on the part of the young person, and the timing and level of support will be crucial. One question that tutors could pose is 'How is what I am doing today helping them to do this independently tomorrow?' Whether it is researching job opportunities or finding information on college courses or training providers, the young person should always be engaged fully in the process so that he or she will be able to move towards independence in the future.
- Tutors must allow young people to 'ride their own bike' in order to enable them to move towards greater independence. This includes allowing them to 'fall off' and being there with the 'sticking plaster' when they need it, such as support when a job interview has not gone well or the young person does not get the college place they wanted.
- Tutors need to work towards a time when the young person no longer needs them: in other words, always trying to do themselves out of a job! Over time, support needs to be gradually withdrawn, to allow the young person to succeed alone. This ensures that young people do not become dependent on others but make a gradual move towards independence – a major indicator that they have reached adulthood.

A tutorial model for CLD

In the ZPD, people learn about career through active participation and discussion with others. Tutors need to consider the ways in which this can be encouraged when supporting young people. In order to learn how to ride a bike, everyone needs opportunities to practise and to play an active part in the learning process. Figure 2.1 shows a tutorial model for CLD.

The model begins at the top of the cycle (Do), and this will often involve a task or an activity that young people carry out either on their own or with others, usually with some support. They then have a discussion with their tutor (Discuss), which gives them the opportunity to think about what they did by describing it, including what they found easy and/or difficult about it, what they enjoyed and/or did not enjoy and so on. This enables young people to begin the process of reviewing and evaluating what they have learned (Review and Evaluate). The tutor then helps young people to focus on their next steps or what they are now ready to do. The tutorial model can be used during one-to-one sessions or in group tutorials.

It is important to remember that those supporting young people can provide them with a safe space in which to participate, where risks can be taken in an atmosphere that promotes trust, confidence and self-reliance. By fostering a culture of participation, young people will begin to construct their own career in interactions with others and learn skills that can be taken forward into all areas of adult life. This will enable them to gain vital

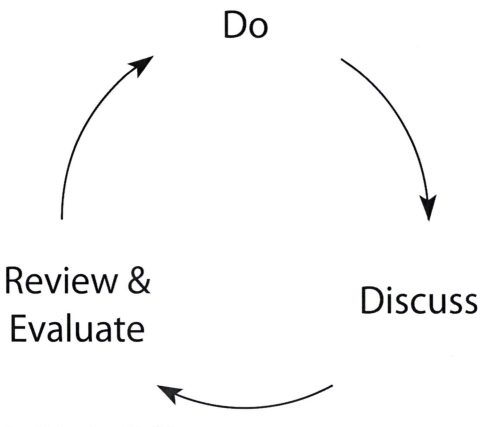

Figure 2.1 A tutorial model for CLD

skills that can be used in the future, when they need to continue to construct their career independently.

Tutors can also provide young people with the 'grass' on which to practise riding their bikes safely. These could be training programmes designed to prepare people for the world of work or work experience while still at school. It is important to maximise the learning that such experiences offer, for example through discussions that enable young people to construct more knowledge in relation to career. Tutors can pose questions such as 'What did you learn about yourself that you didn't know before?' and 'What action can you now take?' to enable them to construct more knowledge about themselves

Conclusion

In this chapter, we have discussed a wide range of approaches for teaching and supporting CLD. In the next chapter, we move on to examine effective curriculum planning and development.

Chapter 3

Curriculum development

Introduction

In this chapter, we look at embedding CLD in the curriculum through collaborative design, planning and development. 'Embedding' takes time, energy and determination. Bolted-on careers activities have less impact and can more easily be squeezed out by competing curriculum priorities. Integrated activities, on the other hand, ensure a rich and expansive learning experience for young people.

CLD in the curriculum

CLD can be embedded in different parts of the curriculum in order to benefit students to the full. Effective CLD will often involve collaborating with students, parents, staff, employers, education partners and other key stakeholders in order to shape a successful programme. The subsequent box shows some of the key opportunities for CLD within the curriculum and highlights some of the challenges these might present.

CLD OPPORTUNITIES IN THE WHOLE CURRICULUM

Opportunities

Information and communication channels

Examples

- School online careers library
- School e-newsletter
- Displays
- Assemblies
- Texts
- Tweets
- Videos and podcasts.

Issues to consider

- Supports independent study and flipped classroom activities.
- Information and communications are selected and quality-assured by the school.

- Messages can be communicated quickly and in a timely way.
- Does not take away time from the subject timetable.
- Students need to be motivated first to use information sources.
- Less effective unless integrated with careers education and guidance activities.
- Helps to inform students, parents, staff and other career influencers about the careers programme.

Opportunities

Assessments and tests

Examaples

- Interest and skills questionnaires
- Aptitude tests
- Psychometric assessments
- Online guidance systems.

Issues to consider

- Supports objective matching processes but can give the illusion that it is a total solution.
- Most useful when students are prepared and followed up, which may require curriculum time.
- Many tests and assessment tools, especially those that are accessed online, have powerful additional features that hardly get used.
- The benefits of using these tests and tools can be squandered if protocols are not in place for sharing the results with all those who work closely with the students who have taken them.

Opportunities

Professional/specialist careers advice on education, training and employment matters:

Examples

- Individual interviews, mentoring and coaching sessions (in person and online)
- Small-group work
- Informal discussion
- Class-sized groups.

Issues to consider

- Individual and small-group work may involve withdrawal from lessons.
- Supports personalised careers education and guidance, but can be expensive to provide.
- Students can be challenged and supported more effectively by professionally-qualified careers staff who are not too close to the student.
- Students benefit from hearing the answers to the questions asked by other students when taking part in a group session.

Opportunities

Non-specialist careers advice (by tutors, peer mentors, parents/carers, employers, trade unionists, etc.) on education, training and employment matters:

Examples

- Individual interviews, mentoring and coaching sessions (in person and online)
- Small-group work
- Informal discussion
- Class-sized groups.

Issues to consider

- Providers may have a holistic view of the young person's needs and can provide opportunities for students to make plans and review their progress.
- Providers may not feel that careers work is their priority.
- Providers are not career experts, but co-learning approaches work well as providers can build up their knowledge alongside the student.
- Helps to involve a wider range of staff in the delivery of the CLD programme.

Opportunities

Learning management processes (target setting, managing progress, etc.)

Examples

- Use of portfolios and e-portfolios for planning, review and reflection
- Action-planning
- Individual learning planning
- Personal development planning.

Issues to consider

- Career planning can be linked to learning plans.
- Helps ensure that learning management is for the benefit of the young person and not just in the interest of the school.
- Helps students to create a career narrative that takes into account their development as learners.
- Strengthens students' motivation and engagement in their own learning.

Opportunities

Formal curriculum interventions include

Examples

- As careers education (i.e. separately-timetabled provision)
- As part of an integrated or composite personal learning and development programme (i.e. careers education linked to elements such as Personal, Social and Health Education (PSHE), citizenship, enterprise education and personal finance education)
- As a cross-curricular theme or enquiry (i.e. taught through subjects and courses).

Issues to consider

- Separate careers education can be easily recognised by students, but, if inadequate time is made available for it, provision may be fragmented and piecemeal.
- The vast scope of some personal learning and development programmes means that topics are sometimes covered superficially.
- Cross-curricular delivery means that the methods, perspectives and forms of explanation of the different subjects can enhance career thinking and understanding, but busy subject teachers may feel under too much pressure to do justice to careers work.
- The formal curriculum provides opportunities for a broad range of teaching approaches such as e-learning, projects, role plays, games and simulations, mini-enterprises, cooperative learning activities, visits (e.g. to colleges, work-based learning providers, universities, workplaces, careers and skills fairs), visitors (e.g. talks, demonstrations and hands-on), work experience and volunteering and work shadowing. The formal curriculum also provides assessment and accreditation possibilities.
- Helps to engage students, parents, staff and other key career influencers in the design, planning, delivery and evaluation of the careers programme.

Opportunities

Extra-curricular and enrichment activities

Examples

- Clubs
- Competitions
- Charity fund-raising
- Sports teams
- Drama and music productions.

Issues to consider

- Enables students to build a career track record and secure positional advantage; but issues related to equality of opportunity must be monitored.
- Provides opportunities for personalising the CLD curriculum but is more difficult to deliver core content this way.
- Helps students who need to have started training already for their chosen career.
- Provides for the possibility of serendipity – students discovering a new career talent or interest.

Opportunities

Incidental and informal learning

Examples

- Transmitted through the ethos of the school
- Peer-to-peer learning.

Issues to consider

- Learning is 'caught' not 'taught' – underlines the importance of staff modelling the behaviour and outlook they want their students to develop.
- Students value 'hot' knowledge over the sometimes 'cold' knowledge of the formal curriculum.
- Shows the importance of building a positive school/college ethos and culture to underpin students' career resilience, happiness and growth.

Curriculum leadership

Choosing and combining different approaches to providing CLD in the curriculum presents a complex challenge, as some parts of the curriculum will be easier to access than others. The curriculum leaders or leadership team for CLD need to focus on the following actions:

- Strategic and long-term actions, for example:

  o Establishing learning intentions for CLD and securing whole-school support for them
  o Communicating and engaging with students, parents, the wider community and other key partners, career influencers and opportunity providers
  o Formalising programmes of study for CLD
  o Negotiating access to opportunities and resources to deliver CLD in and across the curriculum
  o Monitoring, reviewing and evaluating the impact of current CLD provision
  o Facilitating their own professional learning and that of staff involved in the delivery of CLD (see Chapter 7).

- Middle-management and medium-term actions, for example:

  o Producing schemes of work for specific units or modules
  o Reporting on learner progress and achievement.

- Delivery and short-term actions, for example:

  o Producing lesson plans including choosing and developing activities and materials
  o Recording progress and achievement.

Strategic and long-term actions

In order to achieve career growth, become career resilient and strive for career happiness, students need some essential knowledge, skills and attitudes. In this book, we take the view that identifying worthwhile learning intentions and outcomes should involve collaboration between key influencers, partners and stakeholders.

Working with learning outcomes (LOs)

We need to recognise the following:

- Enabling young people to achieve worthwhile outcomes through both formal and informal learning ensures that their CLD is not left to chance.

- Demonstrating the efficacy of a LO approach is challenging. Some results may not show up until many years later, and it is difficult to separate out the impact of different influences and interventions on an individual's progress, achievements and destinations.
- Focusing on planned LOs should not be at the expense of unexpected learning gains that learners may make. It is our belief that teachers should be encouraged as far as is possible in the school system in which they work to use students' responses, individually and collaboratively, to drive the content, methods and outputs of the CLD programme.

We start with an existing framework which can be adapted as necessary as a practical way of developing a set of LOs that are appropriate in the particular context. Various countries have adopted statutory or non-statutory national frameworks. In England, schools are now free to choose their own preferred approach. The international, all-age Blueprint framework of career management competencies is helpful and has been adapted for use in England (Learning and Skills Improvement Service [LSIS], 2012). Another perspective is offered by the *ACEG Framework for Careers and Work-Related Education* (Career Development Institute [CDI], 2012) which provides a progressive framework of LOs for 7- to 19-year-olds based around three strands and 17 areas of learning (see Table 3.1). It suggests measurable outcomes around which careers practitioners can build activities and assessments, and which can substantially contribute to young people's career growth, resilience and happiness.

Table 3.1 Progression in the areas of career and work-related learning from Key Stage 3 to P16

Developing yourself through careers and work-related education

Aspects of learning	Key Stage 3 (KS3)	Key Stage 4 (KS4)	P16
Self-awareness	Describe yourself, your strengths and preferences	Recognise how you are changing, what you have to offer and what's important to you	Assess how you are changing and be able to match your skills, interests and values to requirements and opportunities in learning and work
Self-determination	Tell your own story about what you are doing to make progress, raise your achievement and improve your well-being	Be positive about your own story and the responsibility you are taking for your own progress, achievement and well-being	Create positive accounts of your own story emphasising the responsibility you are taking for managing your own progress, achievement and well-being
Self-improvement as a learner	Explain how you have benefited as a learner from career and work-related learning activities and experiences	Review and reflect upon how you have benefited as a learner from career and work-related learning activities and experiences	Be proactive in taking part in career and work-related learning activities and assessing the benefits to you as a learner

Table 3.1 (Continued)

Learning about careers and the world of work

Aspects of learning	KS3	KS4	P16
Exploring careers and career development	Describe different ways of looking at people's careers and how they develop	Explain key ideas about career and career development	Explain the impact of changing career processes and structures on people's experience and management of their own career development
Investigating work and working life	Identify different kinds of work and why people's satisfaction with their working lives varies	Explain how work is changing and how this impacts on people's satisfaction with their working lives	Recognise the personal, social and economic value of different kinds of work and be critically aware of key debates about the future of work
Understanding business and industry	Describe the organisation and structure of different types of businesses	Explain different types of businesses, how they operate and how they measure success	Explain how what businesses do, the way they operate and the way they measure success are changing
Investigating jobs and labour market information (LMI)	Be aware of what job and LMI is and what it can do for you	Find relevant job and LMI and know how to use it in your career planning	Draw conclusions from researching and evaluating relevant job and LMI to support your future plans
Valuing equality, diversity and inclusion	Identify how to stand up to stereotyping and discrimination that is damaging to you and those around you	Recognise and challenge stereotyping, discrimination and other barriers to equality, diversity and inclusion; know your rights and responsibilities in relation to these issues	Reflect critically on the ethical, legal and business case for equality, diversity and inclusion in the workplace and the implications for your behaviour and others
Learning about safe working practices and environments	Be aware of the laws and by-laws relating to young people's permitted hours and types of employment; know how to minimise health and safety risks to you and those around you	Be aware of your responsibilities and rights as a student, trainee or employee for following safe working practices	Recognise different levels of risk and understand your responsibilities and rights as a student, trainee or employee for observing safe working practices

Table 3.1 (Continued)

Developing your career management and employability skills

Aspects of learning	KS3	KS4	P16
Making the most of careers information, advice and guidance	Identify and make the most of your personal networks of support including how to access the impartial careers information, advice and guidance that you need	Build and make the most of your personal networks of support including making effective use of impartial careers information, advice and guidance	Develop and make the most of your personal networks of support and show that you are a proactive and discerning user of impartial careers information, advice and guidance
Preparing for employability	Recognise the qualities and skills needed for employability and provide evidence for those you have demonstrated both in and out of school	Show that you have acquired and developed qualities and skills to improve your employability	Explain what you are doing to improve your employability and to meet the expectations of employers and co-workers
Showing initiative and enterprise	Recognise when you are using the qualities and skills you need to be enterprising	Show that you can be enterprising in the way you learn, carry out work and plan your career	Develop and apply enterprising qualities and skills in your approach to learning, work and career planning
Developing personal financial capability	Show that you can manage a personal budget and contribute to household and school budgets	Show that you can manage your own money, understand personal financial documents and know how to access financial support for further study and training	Develop your personal financial capability to improve the decisions you make that affect your everyday living, further study, training and work
Identifying choices and opportunities	Look systematically at the choices and opportunities open to you when you reach a decision point	Research your education, training, apprenticeship, employment and volunteering options including information about the best progression pathways through to specific goals	Research and evaluate progression pathways and return on investment for the higher and further education, training, apprenticeship, employment and volunteering options that are open to you
Planning and deciding	Know how to negotiate and make plans and decisions carefully to help you get the qualifications, skills and experience you need	Know how to make important plans and decisions carefully including how to solve problems and deal appropriately with influences on you	Know how to make career-enhancing plans and decisions
Handling applications and selection	Know how to prepare and present yourself well when going through a selection process	Know your rights and responsibilities in a selection process and the strategies to use to improve your chances of being chosen	Know how to prepare for, perform well and learn from your participation in selection processes
Managing changes and transitions	Show that you can be positive, flexible and well prepared at transition points in your life	Review and reflect on previous transitions to help you improve your preparation for future moves in education, training and employment	Know how to develop and use the strategies you will need to cope with the challenges of managing your career transitions

The framework can be used in practice to negotiate, map and audit provision. The template depicted in Table 3.2, for example, can be developed to audit whether the current programme provides sufficient opportunities for the selected outcomes to be achieved. Other subjects/departments can also be asked to indicate how they can contribute to the school's career learning goals.

Table 3.2 Template for CLD audit

Year 9 students will be able to access these LOs ...	... through these learning experiences
• Know how to prepare and present yourself well when going through a selection process	• CV writing and interview role play in English
	• 'Mock' job interviews arranged with the support of local employers
	• Video clips and exercises on the careers area of the school VLE

Mapping can be extended to include an examination of other frameworks (e.g. for PSHE and citizenship) and also against key principles such as equality of opportunity and social justice. However, the actual experience for the learner may not always match the neatness of the planning, and it is important to assess the achievement of the outcomes (see Chapter 2).

Another important application of learning frameworks is to provide continuity, coherence and progression for learners as they move through the school. The subsequent box shows an example of how this can be achieved.

EXAMPLE – *ACEG FRAMEWORK FOR CAREERS AND WORK-RELATED EDUCATION, CDI,* 2012

Theme – self-determination

By age 11, learners will be able to: 'talk positively about what you would like to do' (p. 9).

By age 14, learners will be able to: 'tell your own story, being positive about what you are doing to boost your own progress, achievements and well-being' (p. 11).

By age 16, learners will be able to: 'be positive about your own story showing the responsibility you are taking for your own progress, achievements and well-being' (p. 12).

By age 18, learners will be able to: 'create positive accounts of your own story emphasising the responsibility you are taking for managing your own progress, achievements and well-being' (p. 14).

Learners' needs

LO frameworks can assist in the identification of learners' needs. They are particularly suited to capturing common developmental needs, e.g. that all young people need to be able to make well-informed decisions; but they also can give learners access to public concepts and language that will help them to articulate their own specific needs. The subsequent box contains a checklist of areas for enquiry to help schools identify specific CLD needs and to evaluate the extent to which their current provision meets those needs.

A CHECKLIST FOR SPECIFIC CLD NEEDS

The inner life of the individual

- Personal qualities and temperament
- Values and attitudes
- Interests
- Aptitudes
- Aspirations.

The individual's life situation

- Parental support
- Relationships
- Health
- Social capital: bonding and bridging (Putnam, 2000)
- Cultural capital (Bourdieu, 1986)
- Positional advantage (experiences and achievements and networks of support)
- Learning needs.

The socio-economic environment

- Participation rates in education, training and employment, including apprenticeships
- Local youth labour market.

Collaborative curriculum approaches

It is important to be clear why the CLD curriculum should be negotiated with students themselves and with external partners such as parents and employers. Careers work operates at the interface between the individual and society. Learning about career needs to include an understanding of society and some recognition of the responsibility to the wider society that career brings.

Parents are often part of the local community and therefore are also often part of the local labour market. They are also almost certainly the most powerful influence in the lives, choices and aspirations of their children (ResearchBods, 2012). The following key issues will be raised by involving parents in developing the CLD curriculum:

- Aspiration – schools and parents need to see eye to-eye on raising aspirations and not allowing young people's horizons to be limited by their gender, ethnicity or social background. It is also about negotiating tricky issues with parents who under-aspire, and conversely those who over-aspire, for their children.
- Opportunities – schools and parents need to share their knowledge of opportunities for young people and plug the gaps that each may have. This could include course choices, funding streams, training programmes and employment opportunities.
- Career resilience, happiness and growth – schools and parents need a clear understanding of how the curriculum nurtures young people and what their roles and responsibilities are.
- Networks of support – schools and parents need to use their networks to provide information, advice and access to opportunities. Just as schools provide opportunities for students from other schools (for example in their sixth forms), parents can also be a resource and provide opportunities for other people's children.
- Lifestyle choices and balances – schools and parents need to open a dialogue about lifestyle choices and values and how these should be accommodated in the CLD curriculum.

The CLD curriculum should also be developed collaboratively with internal partners in the school community. Schools and colleges are often the largest local employer. When we consider who is employed by such institutions, we may well immediately think of teachers. However, there is also a wide range of other people who work in them too, e.g. administrators, caterers, grounds people and maintenance engineers, accounts experts, health professionals, technicians, security guards and not forgetting careers advisers. Even amongst the teaching staff, there will be individuals with fascinating career stories from the past that can inspire young people. Staff also have access to networks which, as we pointed out previously in relation to parents, can be of advantage to the whole school community.

Students have an important part to play in the design, delivery and evaluation of CLD provision. Most public education systems emphasise the importance of preparing young people for the opportunities, responsibilities and experiences of later life (Department for Education in England [DfE], 2013). Signatories to the United Nations Convention on the Rights of the Child (UNCRC), 1989 (DfE, 2012), such as the United Kingdom, accept that all children have the right to say what they think in all matters affecting them and to have their views taken seriously (Article 12). For this reason, students should be at the centre of the design, delivery and evaluation of CLD provision. The alternative, providing a programme that is centrally designed, instils a 'top-down' approach that can distance the individual learner from the learning and undermine the engagement of those learners with the programme. Ensuring the engagement of young people with the design, delivery and evaluation of a programme can feed into an annual process of evaluation so that the evaluation of one year is fed into the design and delivery of the next.

Collaborative curriculum planning can revive an inherited and unexamined careers programme. Inertia and false confidence that 'if it ain't broken don't fix it' can allow the careers programme to become out of date, unresponsive and ineffective. Talking to learners about their needs and priorities and engaging with their key career influencers (parents, other staff, employers, etc.) can significantly improve the design, delivery and impact of the CLD programme. The checklist and suggestions in the subsequent box will assist the process.

COLLABORATIVE CURRICULUM PLANNING CHECKLIST

- Discuss relevant school performance data with senior leaders. Identify how the CLD programme can help to address any issues that exist, e.g. those related to attendance and behaviour, inclusion, socio-economic disadvantage, raising aspirations, underachievement (boys/girls/ethnic minorities), progression, retention, achievement and destinations.
- Meet with local business leaders and organisations, human resources (HR) and training managers, apprenticeship providers and governors to identify trends and opportunities for your learners in local and national labour markets. Find out how your school can help them, e.g. opportunities for community engagement and development opportunities for their staff. Discuss what they could offer your learners, e.g. work experience placements, competitions and challenges, visits and visitors, mentors, support in running business simulations and activities to develop enterprise and employability skills, assisting learners with project work.
- Arrange focus groups and surveys of parents and carers to find out what concerns they have and how well they think current careers provision is meeting their children's needs. Discuss ways they can help other parents' children, e.g. by taking part in a careers fair. Organise or ask to be involved in evenings for parents, e.g. to discuss their children's subject choices, to find out about HE options and finance and to discuss ways of helping their children with planning and deciding.

Develop the sustained involvement of learners in identifying and finding solutions to the real issues that affect their career learning, e.g. through tutor group discussions, focus groups, small-scale surveys, School Council–led enquiries (or other student decision-making bodies), action research and student conferences. Consider appointing a careers champion in each tutor group who can be trained to deliver aspects of the careers programme and provide feedback on the impact of the overall programme. Other methods include using texts, emails, forums, suggestion boxes and graffiti walls.

It is very important when extending 'ownership' of the CLD programme to give both staff and students time and support to develop their roles, build trust in the process and gain confidence in what they are doing.

Resources and opportunities

At the senior level, leaders are responsible for identifying, evaluating, increasing and effectively deploying resources needed to deliver the CLD curriculum.

The spectrum of careers resources that need to be made available ranges from published learning materials produced by careers professionals to opportunities offering direct experience, for example:

- Books, booklets, information sheets, posters (printed or online)
- Broadcasts, video clips
- Textbooks, workbooks

- Software and websites
- Business simulations, games and role plays
- Speakers and visitors from education and industry (including members of your own staff and parents/carers)
- Visits out including careers and skills fairs and taster days
- Work shadowing and work experience.

It is useful to take stock of what you are using annually in order to check for quality and value for money. You can also take the opportunity to carry out a survey of new resources and spot resources that are being underused or that could be replaced.

Monitoring, review and evaluation

Senior leaders need to make decisions about what needs to be monitored, reviewed and evaluated to ensure that the CLD curriculum is well planned, continues to improve and is fit for purpose. When considering whether or not a programme is fit for purpose, it is worth considering each of the elements in the EFFE model (Chapter 1).

Tips for developing an effective strategy include the following:

- Have a clear focus for the evaluation, for example:
  - o Are students progressing further than might be expected considering the particular school's intake?
  - o Do all students have appropriate next steps, and are they equipped and willing to take them?
  - o Are inputs and access sufficient, e.g. in terms of curriculum time, staffing levels, resources, numbers of interview and group work sessions held?
  - o How well does the provision enable students to achieve career-related skills?
  - o What is the impact of the CLD programme on students' career growth, resilience and happiness skills?

- Do not try to evaluate everything you do. Identify a clear trigger for what you want to evaluate (e.g. you are not sure whether a particular approach or intervention is working).
- Consider the return on investment before committing yourself to an evaluation project (e.g. there is little point in doing an evaluation if you cannot put the findings and recommendations before decision makers and influence change).
- Involve those who will be the focus of the evaluation from the outset, including the students themselves, to gain their support for what you are doing.
- Use an evaluation planner, e.g. What is the focus of the evaluation? Why is it a concern? What are your hypotheses or main ideas in relation to the focus of the evaluation? Who will be involved? What will it cost? How will data be collected? How will the data collection instruments be piloted? How will the data be analysed? How will the results be used? How will the results be presented and disseminated?

Table 3.3 outlines the main advantages and disadvantages of the principal methods of data collection. Methods can be used singly or, where appropriate, in combination to increase the robustness of the evaluation study.

Table 3.3 Principal methods of data collection

Method of data collection	Notes
Observations Decide type: • Unstructured, e.g. a natural observation of a lesson • Structured, e.g. using a schedule or pre-coded checklist	• Useful for monitoring relationships and interactions • Simple to record observations on a sheet on a clipboard, but video recording can reveal more data and be used with participants after the event, e.g. to validate the observation • The observer must be careful not to inhibit participants by their presence • The analysis may be complex
Interviews Decide type: • Structured: follows a fixed or predetermined set of questions • Semi-structured: a set of questions has been prepared in advance, but the interviewer can add supplementary questions to follow up or explore further the interviewee's responses • Unstructured: the scope of the interview is not predetermined in advance Interviews can be: • One-to-one • Group, e.g. a focus group	• Useful for in-depth probing of the feelings and opinions of key actors in a situation • Respondents are free to use their own words • Interviews can be more time-consuming than administering questionnaires • Structured interviews may not allow you to achieve more than you could with a questionnaire • Use semi-structured interviews if you want to collect some common information from all respondents but want the scope to allow respondents to say different things • Unstructured interviews involving several respondents can be difficult to analyse
Questionnaires Formats include: • Tick-box (closed question type) • Stem statements (unfinished sentences – open question type) • Free comment (open question type) • Use of scales, i.e. respondents rate or rank their responses	• Useful for satisfaction surveys, asking for suggestions where anonymity might be an advantage • Useful for processing large numbers relatively quickly • Can be used to identify a sample for more detailed follow-up, e.g. by interview • Errors can creep in if respondents misunderstand the questions • Important to pilot the questionnaire to make sure the questions and the layout are clear and unambiguous
Documentary evidence Documents may be: • Pre-existing documents which have not been specially created for the purposes of the evaluation • Specially created artefacts for the purpose of the evaluation • Products which have come into being naturally during the course of the evaluation Examples: • Diaries/logs • Agendas and minutes • Correspondence • Reports • Statistics	• Useful for finding out the views and ideas of the principal actors in a situation • Use of pre-existing documents can save respondents having to create information just for the evaluation • Pre-existing documentation may not cover all the information needed • Information may be difficult to analyse

The analysis and interpretation of data is a vital stage in the evaluation process. The methods to be used will have been decided at the planning stage and could include the following:

- Statistical analysis, e.g. tallies, percentages, distribution and cross-tabulation
- Qualitative analysis, e.g. indexing, coding and charting
- Deductive analysis – using predetermined categories derived from theory
- Inductive analysis – discovering categories, dimensions, etc. from the data.

The dissemination strategy should also have been agreed to at the planning stage to maximise the chances of the evaluation having the effect intended. Useful tips include the following:

- Tailor what you include in your report to your audience
- Only include necessary information
- Be transparent
- Provide an executive summary
- Only use important results – be discriminating.

As well as strategic-level planning and evaluation, medium- and short-term planning and evaluation are important for improving the effectiveness of provision.

Middle management and medium-term actions

Creating schemes of work for units or modules is an important level of planning between the overview of a programme of study and the fine detail of a lesson plan. It enables you to do the following:

- Keep sight of the overarching aims of your CLD provision, i.e. promoting career resilience, happiness and growth.
- Bridge the gap between the broader and longer term outcomes identified in your learning framework and the detailed and specific outcomes in your lesson plans.
- Check the levels of learning that students will be able to access. CV writing, for example, can become a utilitarian, box-filling exercise. A well-considered scheme of work should stimulate reflective learning, e.g. how can I consistently produce CVs from now on that have a maximum impact on their recipient?
- Examine the balance of different learning and assessment activities over the period of the unit or module.

An example of a scheme of work for introducing students to labour market information (LMI) is shown subsequently.

Scheme of work – module title, 'My LMI Teaching Group: Y9S'

Overview

This module (6 x 60 minutes) aims to show students what LMI is, how to find it and how to turn it into useful information that will improve their decisions about what to study next year, as well as help their long-term career planning. It will help them tackle well-known issues related to the availability, accessibility and analysis of careers-related LMI. Students complete a short LMI investigation of their own and find out how LMI provides insight into progress in promoting equality in different occupations which could be relevant to their needs and interests.

Intended LOs

LO 7 from The ACEG Framework for Careers and Work-Related Education is 'to be aware of what job and LMI is and what it can do for you' (CDI, 2012: 11).

Cross-curricular links

Cross-curricular links include English (comprehension), maths (statistics), geography (location of industry), PSHE and citizenship (equality and diversity).

Table 3.4 Lesson schedule

Lesson no./ duration/date	Content	Outcomes Students are able to:	Activities (including assessment) Students:
1	• What is LMI and why is it important to employers and to individuals who can offer their labour? • Making choices with and without up-to-date and reliable LMI • Issues related to finding, distilling and using LMI (turning LMI into My LMI)	• Define LMI • Explain the importance of using LMI to inform their decisions • Identify ways of dealing with problems related to the provision of careers LMI	• Analyse case studies of choices made by individuals in a range of work settings • Extract the key messages from three short pieces of information about trends and opportunities in architecture • Review their learning and progress in a short plenary
2	• Understanding the local labour market – opportunities, trends and forecasts • Where to find local LMI	• Describe key employment features of their local economy • Identify sources of local LMI	• Complete a virtual industry trail and answer questions on it as they go along • Analyse vacancies on local job-seeker and newspaper websites • Browse LMI resources on school VLE • Review their learning and progress in a short plenary
3	• The national labour market – trends and forecasts • Understanding skills-related issues (e.g. the hourglass economy, how a lack of skills restricts individuals to the secondary labour market, how job seekers can be unable to utilise their skills as a result of taking qualifications that are not recognised or as a result of being overspecialised)	• Identify major trends in employment in the United Kingdom • Understand the importance of developing their skills and gaining recognised qualifications	• Take part in a true-or-false quiz based on trends and forecasts in the UK economy • Process and analyse carefully selected raw data on skills and present their findings graphically, e.g. using line graphs, bar graphs and pie graphs • Review their learning and progress in a short plenary

4	• Carrying out a mini-project to investigate an aspect of LMI that interests them (a project brief will be provided with suggested resources)	• Identify a topic to investigate that is relevant to their needs
		• Use information skills to carry out the investigation
		• Manage and successfully complete a small-scale project
			• Begin their investigations, singly or in groups, into an aspect of LMI that is of particular interest to them, for example:
			  o Related to a specific occupation (such as who are the main employers, where are the jobs located, earnings, competition for entry and supply and demand)
			  o Related to a specific subject (such as the short- and medium-term destinations of English graduates)
			  o Related to employers' expectations (such as actual as opposed to minimum entry requirements, skills and employability requirements)
			• Finish off their mini-projects for homework and prepare their presentations for lesson six (to be uploaded on the school VLE afterwards)

5	• Identifying barriers to equality of opportunity in specific sectors of the labour market, e.g. architecture, politics • Finding out how segregation, stereotyping and inequality are being tackled in different sectors of the labour market, e.g. in the Science, Technology, Engineering and Maths (STEM) industries, accountancy	• Identify key factors in labour market inequalities • Identify how to recognise and challenge unfairness • Identify how to thrive despite the existence of obstacles in the labour market	• Discuss reports in the news that show how some employers are failing to access all the talent available to them (e.g. by only recruiting from a narrow range of universities) and make recommendations for tackling the problems they have discussed • Draw up a list of skills that will help individuals to be more adaptable and resilient when they encounter obstacles in the labour market
6	• Students make short presentations to each other based on their LMI mini-project reports	• Explain and make their findings accessible to an audience of their peers	• Make two- to three-minute presentations to the class • Students give each other supportive feedback on their presentations

Delivery and short-term actions

Lesson plans

Better Practice – A Guide to Delivering Effective Career Learning 11–19 reminds us that 'learning cannot take place unless young people know what they are learning and why, and what they are expected to achieve' (Donoghue, 2008:62). Where possible, it can help students find flow if they can work out the relevance for themselves and write about how a lesson has impacted their lives. Well-structured lesson plans, therefore, are particularly important. The subsequent box explains the template used for the lesson plans in this guide.

SUGGESTED HEADINGS FOR A LESSON-PLANNING TEMPLATE

Teaching group

Date/duration

Title overview

Curriculum links and standards

LOs

- By the end of the session, students will be able to:

Resources/materials

Preparation

Activities (with approximate timings)

- Introduction
- Main activities and methods and techniques used (includes information about differentiation/personalisation)
- Plenary

Assessment/homework

Notes for learning support assistant

Extension ideas

Review notes

Student involvement in the design, delivery and evaluation of CLD provision

We conclude this chapter with an examination of the importance of involving students in the process of designing, delivering and evaluating CLD. The idea of hearing and acting upon the 'student voice' is underpinned by the general principles of the United Nations Convention of Rights of the Child (UNCRC), – Articles 2, 3, 6 and, in particular, Article 12 (DfE, 2012). Within the context of education, there are other equally powerful arguments for including the ideas and suggestions of young people in the design and delivery of learning. Much of the learning that takes place in CLD is of a personal nature in that it often focuses on the development of self-knowledge. So being sure to hear and act on the student voice is of paramount importance.

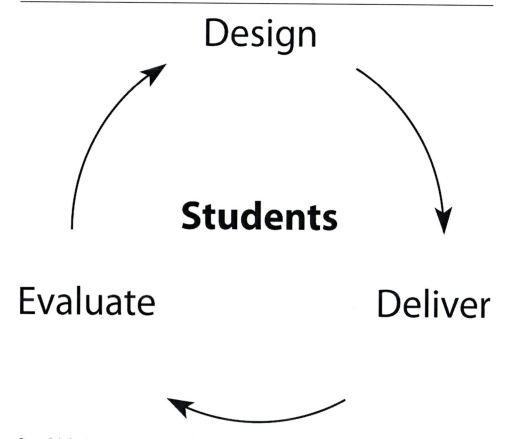

Figure 3.1 Students at the centre of the curriculum

The intended outcomes for career learning, unlike many other areas of learning, are specific to individuals and are affected by the context of the students. Students need to be at the centre of the design, delivery and evaluation of CLD provision as it is all about them. The alternative (providing a programme that is centrally designed by instilling a 'top-down' approach) can distance students from the learning, undermine the engagement of those learners with the programme and ultimately runs the risk of failing to meet their needs. Involving young people with the design, delivery and evaluation of a programme (see Figure 3.1) can go a long way to facilitating their engagement in an ongoing way.

All aspects of the CLD programme must promote career resilience, happiness and growth and provide opportunities to develop skills towards them. Encouraging and enabling young people to be at the heart of the design and delivery of a programme can do just that. During this process, they will encounter the need for resilience when they hear different (and perhaps opposing) viewpoints to their own, and have access to opportunities for growth and development in relation to a variety of skills. Later they will be able to reflect on their own personal experience of the process and how satisfied they are with the outcomes. Placing young people at the centre of the evaluation of a programme gives them responsibility, respects their views and affirms the importance of the programme itself.

In relation to the involvement of young people, Treseder (1997) presents a helpful model that illustrates five levels of participation and describes the degree of involvement of young people in decisions that affect them at each level. He recognises that there will be some decisions and processes that young people are not equipped to take responsibility for, and others where they can have more control. Each of the levels is described subsequently, with an example of how this could be done in the context of CLD.

Assigned but informed: an activity or programme is designed by a career professional or obtained from a publication and cross-referenced against the appropriate framework for career learning. The delivery is planned by the professionals, but young people are informed about its relevance and asked for their thoughts and feedback afterwards.

Adult-initiated, shared decisions with young people: an activity or programme is initially planned and designed by the professional, but its implementation involves young people in decisions about content, timing and modes of delivery.

Young people initiated and directed: this requires a forum for young people's ideas to be voiced, such as a student council, or student representation on a curriculum development team. Alternatively it may be that such ideas emerge from active participation of young people in the evaluation of a programme. An example could be the establishment of a career page or University Open Day page on a school intranet. This could be managed and written by the students, so that when someone attends an Open Day they can add it to the page. The school or an individual member of staff would oversee such a project to ensure that it adhered to the law and did not infringe individual rights to privacy but would not manage or control it.

Young people–initiated, shared decisions with adults: as discussed previously, this would be an initiative that has come directly from the young people themselves but that requires adult support in order to implement it. Decisions are shared between the young people and the adults, but adults do not dominate. For example, young people might like to run a virtual or even a real business. The complexities of such an endeavour mean that it would be difficult for the young people to do this without adult support and advice.

Young people consulted and informed: adults design and deliver a programme or activity, but the young people are consulted at every stage of the process, and their ideas are respected and considered fully. For example, a focus group of young people could be formed to help plan and organise a job or HE fair. As well as ensuring that young people's voices are heard and responded to, active participation in this means that the young people concerned are using and developing important skills, as well as benefitting from the end result.

Conclusion

In this chapter, we have discussed a wide range of approaches for curriculum design. In Part II, we will explore a range of CLD activities for students of different age groups.

Part II

Facilitating CLD

Chapter 4

CLD 11–14

Introduction

The next three chapters focus on facilitating CLD across the 11–19 age range. Each chapter suggests ways of helping students to achieve career resilience, happiness and growth. This chapter looks at the needs of 11- to 14-year-olds.

Supporting self-awareness and career exploration remain the bedrock of CLD activities for this age group, although preparing young people to make educational choices and decisions is an important requirement of many education systems. At the younger end of the age range, many career ideas will still be based on wishful thinking (Howard and Walsh, 2011).

Activities that help students to appreciate what different jobs are about, the skills required and the amount of education and training involved will widen their horizons and help them begin to think about their own interests, values and capacities. Some young people who are already committed to career-building activities such as intensive sports training may need additional support. Raising aspirations and challenging stereotypes remain key priorities to stop young people from ruling out a range of possibilities for themselves (Peterson, Rollins and Thomas, 1985). These years are critical in young people's or ientation towards a unique personal identity (Gottfredson, 1981). Activities that enable young people to achieve and succeed in key life roles and domains (e.g. in family life, school life, citizenship/volunteering and leisure) help young people to understand who they are and who they possibly could become. It is also an important time to raise their awareness of the rewards and responsibilities of working life and the unpredictability of labour markets.

Career resilience

Raising awareness

RISKS AND REWARDS

You can introduce the concept of resilience by exploring how the different attitudes of individuals to success and failure can affect their willingness to take risks. Resilient individuals are more likely to be receptive to the idea of taking risks if they are confident in their ability to bounce back from failure.

Ask students to get into groups of four and have each tell the others about a risk that he or she has taken, what the 'prize' was and whether it was worth the risk. Provide some examples to help them get started, such as the following.

School

1. Joining an after school activity that none of your friends are part of

    Risk – alienating friends, being on your own at the activity
    Prize – doing something you're interested in, making new friends, learning new
    skills

2. Walking home alone in the dark

    Risk – jeopardizing personal safety, getting into trouble with parents
    Prize – feeling independent, saving bus fare, doing something daring

3. Asking a question in a lesson when everyone seems to understand except you

    Risk – looking foolish, irritating the teacher, drawing attention to yourself
    Prize – understanding so you do better in the lesson, in your homework and in
    the exam

Work

4. Putting yourself forward for a promotion

    Risk – not getting it and looking foolish, 'too big for your own boots' or overly
    ambitious
    Prize – getting it and looking ambitious, positive and willing to learn

5. Volunteering for a special project or to attend a meeting

    Risk – ending up with a lot of extra work, not managing it well, being seen as 'a
    creep'
    Prize – gaining broader experience, expertise and knowledge, being seen as a
    positive and forward-looking person

6. Taking a problem or dispute to senior managers on behalf of the team

    Risk – being labelled a troublemaker by senior managers, ending up with a lot of
    extra work and responsibility
    Prize – being recognised by senior managers as a leader, someone who cares
    about the team morale and has clear values

7. Avoiding a task or activity that is part of the job because you don't enjoy it or
    aren't very good at it

    Risk – getting in trouble/being found out, colleagues having low opinion of you
    Prize – having more time to do what you prefer, being seen as bold and a maverick
    by your peers

Developing inner strength and resources

We can help individuals to develop the protective factors that help to mitigate against the risk of career problems at work by rehearsing that risk or adversity within the safety of a CLD setting.
Personal protective factors include the following:

- Developing personal strengths, feelings, beliefs and attitudes, e.g. in relation to risk, problem-solving
- Realistic and honest understanding of self in relation to others, the world of work and of 'my potential'
- Developing social and interpersonal competencies, e.g. assertiveness and negotiation skills, networking skills.

RESILIENCE AND SELF-ACCEPTANCE

Being understanding and accepting of oneself is a major protective factor. Many resources have been created and made available online for you to use to encourage students to feel positive about their appearance, attributes, strengths, differences and interests. Activities that allay young people's anxieties about who they are not only help them to cope with the transition to adulthood but also build resilience for the future.

Stories such as *Beauty and the Beast, Shrek, The Frog Prince* and *The Ugly Duckling* offer a good starting point. The message in all these tales is about discovering and releasing the inner beauty within the individual. Let the students think in pairs about the people they admire the most, like the most and would like to emulate. Are looks the most important thing? Where do character, talent, intelligence and morality come in their judgements?

An exploration of the notion of beauty in the media, in different times and cultures and at different stages of life can boost young people's well-being and resilience. Departments such as drama, textiles, art and history may be able to help here. The topic can be followed up in many different ways, for example:

- Students can discuss the motivation for dressing differently and the risks of being ostracised (individual versus collective identity).
- Job seekers who are rejected by employers because they don't fit the image of the organisation (aesthetic labour).
- Individuals who are happy to wear uniforms and those who would turn down a job that involved wearing a uniform (the symbolic and practical purposes of work clothes).

Find pictures of young people wearing 'uniforms', for example a group of young people wearing 'hoodies', or dressed in similar clothing going to a party. Ask the young people to discuss the question 'When is a uniform not a uniform?'

Strengthening external resources and support

Developing resilience is also linked to building networks of support, e.g. family, friends, teachers and other professionals or contacts who can provide emotional support as well as access to information and opportunities.

TEAMWORK

Tell students that they can organise a mini–sports day with simple events such as standing on one leg for the longest time and shooting a ball through the basket. Students get into teams to compete, but for the first time round, do not allow team members to encourage individuals on their side. Record individuals' results and scores.

Run the 'sports day' again, but this time allow the rest of the team to cheer and support individuals on their side. It is important that individuals take part in the same events. Once again, keep a record of individual scores/results.

Now compare the two performances of individuals. How many students did better the second time around? Ask for possible explanations of why this was the case. If the suggestion does not come from the class, ask them to consider the hypothesis that team supporters boost individual resilience. In what other life situations could they try to harness this effect?

Building networks of support

We can teach young people about the strengths of networks so that they can build their own based on their own merits and their own contributions. Making a network map like Ahmed's (see Figure 4.1) or Kathryn's can help students to realise just how many contacts and potential supporters they could have.

Ahmed (age 14) lives with his mother and father, paternal grandfather and grandmother (PGF and PGM, respectively) and maternal grandmother (MGM). He also has a younger brother and an older sister. His sister is soon to be married and will then move in with her husband and his parents and brother a few miles away. Ahmed's

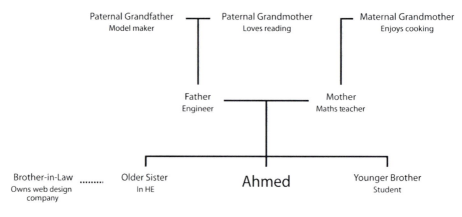

Figure 4.1 Ahmed's network

father is an engineer in a local electronics company, and his mother is a maths teacher at the sixth form college. Other occupations or expertise are indicated in Figure 4.1.

Kathryn (age 18) regularly attends a local youth group run by three local adults. All are volunteers, but they also work as a nurse, a marketing manager, and a tree surgeon. It's a lively and fun environment of between 15 and 20 young people. Currently, they are engaged in two projects in the community. The first is to tidy up small areas of unused land in the town and to plant vegetables for the local community (Growing Project). The other is to organise regular friendship visits to elderly members of the community who live alone (Visiting Project).

Kathryn's network might be described as follows in relation to the new understandings she will gain regarding the world of work and how her skills will develop:

- Through the youth group, Kathryn interacts with people from three different occupational areas – medical, business and marketing and land-based work.
- Through the Growing Project, she learns environmental awareness, gains knowledge of agriculture and horticulture and learns how to work in a team.
- Through the Visiting Project, she develops her communication skills and learns about planning and taking responsibility.

Sample lesson plan for career resilience

Lesson plan template

Teaching group (year group or specific needs group)
Year 7 (Y7)

Date/duration
September
Part of induction into Y7
The length of time will vary from 50 minutes to 2 hours

Title overview
Me, myself, I
This lesson forms the foundation of the development of resilience by encouraging the understanding of and acceptance of themselves. It incorporates elements of risk taking in the activities, revealing thoughts and feelings and possibly volunteering to put on costumes.

Curriculum links and standards (e.g. Personal, Social, Health and Economic Education [PSHEE])

- Self-awareness as part of personal development in PSHEE, history, human geography, and religious studies.

LOs
By the end of the lesson, the students will:

1. Be able to describe at least three different sides to 'me'
2. Have discussed the qualities in others that matter most to me

3. Have explored the subjective nature of 'beauty' or 'attractiveness' and how it varies through history and across cultures
4. Understand that although they will change outwardly there is an essence of 'self' that does not change.

Resources/materials

Preparation:
Song, story, pictures of 'beauty' across culture and history

Activities (with approximate timings):
Introduction/starter (10 minutes)

*   Play 'Me, Myself and I' song by Joan Armatrading.
*   Explain that this is all about 'me'. Whatever we do in life, whoever we are with, one thing we can be sure of is that we will live that life as 'me' – so perhaps we'd better get to know ourselves!
*   Please note: it is important that some ground rules are established about students' comments and revelations.
*   Who am I? List the different 'people' we are, e.g. Joan's daughter, Mark's best mate, Little Jo's babysitter, the student representative in class 7EG. How many descriptions can you come up with? Share them with your neighbour.
*   Discuss the different relationships those descriptions relate to – family, friends, school, 'work'.

Main activities and methods and techniques used (includes information about differentiation/personalisation)

*   Discussion with class: one way that we know ourselves is how we look. But is that how others see us? How important is what we look like in society today? What are the issues or problems associated with an emphasis on looks?
*   If the group dynamics or the ability levels in the class make a general class discussion problematic, then small groups of four could use a diamond nine to rank the importance of looks, wealth, kindness, intelligence, hardworking, reliability, fitness, health, creativity – and explain their reasons. If they don't put 'looks' high up, do they think that our society agrees with them? (10 minutes)
*   In pairs, make a list of famous people, noting what they are famous for and whether we would like to be like them in some way. Write them on the board, and then have a discussion about the most desirable traits.
*   Alternatively, give small groups four pictures of famous people and ask them to write what they are famous for on the back. Ask individuals to say which they would like to be like and why. (15 minutes)
*   Read/refer to the story of *Beauty and the Beast/Shrek/The Ugly Duckling*. In groups of four, decide what the key message(s) is from the story. Time will vary depending on the story and whether you read it out or précis it. (5 minutes)
*   So what is beauty? It might be different in different cultures and at different times in history. Show pictures as examples.
*   Opportunity to 'dress up' in some costumes, e.g. Sari, Georgian-style man's wig. Time will depend on whether dressing up option included or just show pictures and discuss. (minimum of 10 minutes)

Plenary (5 minutes)

- Summarise what has been covered in this lesson – it's all about me, myself and I. What you look like will change a lot over the coming years, but 'you' will still be you. How would you describe the 'you' that won't change? Write one word on a piece of paper and keep it – you don't need to show anyone.

Assessment/homework:

Find an example of a uniform – either a photograph or draw it or bring part of it in. What does it say about the wearer, if anything?

Notes for learning support assistant:

Support in the classroom may be needed to encourage discussion and to get contributions from all of the learners. Care will be needed also to ensure that there are no unchecked inappropriate comments about race/culture or individuals' looks.

Extension ideas:

Research into historical concepts of 'beauty' – present findings as a poster or PowerPoint presentation.

Review notes:

How well did the students engage with the discussions and were the concepts 'self', 'beauty' and 'body image' understood?

Career happiness

Valuing happiness

Young people are unlikely to have given much thought to their career happiness. Activities that help them to understand what career happiness is about will also help them to recognise it and value it.

WHAT IS HAPPINESS?

Ask students to write a statement that would be true if they were completely or mostly happy with their life at school such as 'I enjoy coming to school to be with my friends'. Ask them to discuss some of the statements to understand different dimensions of happiness.
   Develop the activity by:

- Repeating it for different aspects of life, e.g. school work, doing jobs around the home, use of free time, voluntary work, friends, appearance, dream job.
- Selecting ten statements and carrying out a survey of the year group to assess the general level of happiness with school life. (Students answer true or false to each statement.)
- For each statement, asking the class to suggest two or three practical steps that students could take if they wanted to change their answer from false to true.
- Talking about the challenges of asking questions about happiness and designing surveys to measure it.

• Tell the class about how the Children's Happiness scale was constructed (Office for Standards in Education [Ofsted], 2012) and give students the chance to work out their 'happiness score for today'.

Fairy tales

In English lessons, read one of the many stories of the foolish husband who is granted three wishes and plots to use them as a shortcut to riches and happiness (e.g. Charles Perrault's *The Ludicrous Wishes*). He stupidly wastes his wishes and ends up no better off than he was before. The students discuss the moral of the story. Then they write an updated version of the story in a modern setting and put someone like themselves or someone that they know in one of the parts.

Finding inner happiness

Individuals can transform their inner lives by understanding what makes them happy.

THE HIGH FIVE PRINCIPLES

The High Five principles are an important part of the learning in *The Real Game* series (Prospects, 2005). They can be used in their own right to stimulate students' thinking not only about career happiness but also about resilience and growth. These are the principles:

• Follow your heart
• Change is constant
• Learning is ongoing
• Focus on the journey
• Access your allies.

This introduces the concept of career as a journey through life largely made up of the experiences of the different kinds of work students will do on the way. Students use prompt questions to imagine where they will be and what they will be doing in five years' time:

• Where do you see yourself in five years' time?
• How do you think you will change in the next five years and how do you think the world around you will change?
• What would you like to learn to do in the next five years?
• How do you think you will be feeling two years into your five-year journey?
• Who will help you get there and who will you help to get where you want to be?

In the discussion that follows, the session leader links the questions to the High Five principles and brings out the connection between the principles and how students could achieve career growth, happiness and resilience. The idea of focusing on the journey, for example, leads to an interesting debate about whether career happiness is to be found at the end of the journey or on the journey itself. The session leader points out the pitfalls of externalising happiness and making it dependent on outcomes that are outside the control of the individual. That makes it easier to blame other people and situations for their unhappiness. Focusing on the journey reminds us that happiness comes from within ourselves. As Buddha said, 'People often ask me, "What is the way to happiness?" and I reply, "Happiness is the way"'.

At the end of the session, ask students to rate how much the High Five principles had meant to them before today and then to rate how much of an effect they think the principles will have on what they do from now on.

Maximising happiness

Schools can help individuals to maximise their chances of career happiness by cultivating optimism and improving their life situation.

Learned optimism

Respond to research into the benefits of cultivating optimism in young people. Devise a series of exercises to help students improve their explanatory style:

- Begin a discussion on 'framing' by showing a picture of a half-filled glass of water and asking whether it is half full or half empty. Students discuss career situations in which it is easier or more difficult to perceive the glass as half full, e.g. how a person in a poorly-paid job might feel if before they had been unemployed, or if before they had held a well-paid job.
- Explain the difference between an optimistic and a pessimistic explanatory style, and have students give examples related to people's career hopes, e.g. 'I wasn't up to it; that's why they didn't offer me the job' (pessimistic style) versus 'it's their fault if they couldn't see that I'd be brilliant in the job' (optimistic style).
- Students probe the differences between 'realistic' optimism and 'pie in the sky' optimism when setting career goals.
- Ask students to do some improvised drama. Students warm up by adjusting their body language to words that they hear, e.g. confidence, happiness, helplessness, anxiety, despair. Then introduce the scenario which is to explore responses to the loss of middle-level service jobs from the introduction of new technology, e.g. the impact of online retailing on jobs in the high street. Students role-play attending an alumni evening a few years after they have left school. They invent a backstory for themselves in which they have to imagine that they have faced redundancy because new technology (software, robots, etc.) took away their jobs and then imagine what happened next in their careers. Students perform different versions of the alumni evening: one in which they are optimistic about what is happening to them, the other in which they are pessimistic about their situation. Afterwards they reflect on the insights they have gained from the drama.

Gratitude

Refer to recent psychological studies and the teachings of the great religions that suggest that grateful people are happier and more resilient. Ask the class to make a 'gratitude list' in their careers portfolios for one week. Each day, students write down three things that they are grateful for. Encourage the class to make a special effort to say appreciative things to others during the week.

In the next session, give students the opportunity to reflect on their experience. Has expressing gratitude made them feel more positive about themselves and their lives? Have they got on better with other people? Do they feel more in control of their lives?

Extend the discussion to stimulate students' thinking about the role of gratitude in the workplace. The session leader should mention things that happen in professional life, such as being endorsed for their skills on LinkedIn. Does expressing and receiving gratitude improve relationships with colleagues and increase job satisfaction? How important is gratitude in customer care, e.g. thanking customers for buying something from you? How can an organisation change its culture to embrace gratitude?

Lesson plan on career happiness

Teaching group

Date/duration
Two hours

Title overview
Green school
A creative problem-solving exercise for students to design a new green school making use of information that is provided about requirements, costs and the environmental impact of building a new school.

Curriculum links and standards

- 'Explain how you have benefited as a learner from career and work-related learning activities and experiences' (KS3 LO3, *The ACEG Framework for Careers and Work-Related Education*; CDI, 2012:11).
- Cross-curricular links: citizenship, design and technology, environmental education, geography, science.

LOs
By the end of the session, students will be able to:

- Explain how values and attitudes influence decisions and solutions to problems
- Appreciate how sustainable living and working can enhance human happiness and well-being
- Recognise the challenge of changing their own behaviour as students and future workers to work in greener ways
- Recognise that providing goods and services in an environmentally responsible way applies to all sectors of the economy and not just the 'green industries'.

Resources/materials

- Information sheets about the scenario provided on the school VLE
- Links to useful websites
- Experts available for students to consult, e.g. school architect, landscape architect.

Preparation:
Work with school business manager and governors on developing the scenario

Activities (with approximate timings):
Introduction (10 minutes)

- Outline the objectives of the lesson.
- Introduce the scenario. 'We can build a brand-new school on part of our playing fields and pay for it by selling off the old school building to property developers . . . This is a great opportunity to develop a school that has a much lower environmental impact and which will enable us to work in greener ways'.
- Students will work in small groups on making recommendations on developing different aspects of the project before coming together to discuss their suggestions.

Main activities (60 minutes)

- Allocate students between the different groups required:

  o Development of buildings, e.g. architecture, building materials, aesthetic considerations
  o Development of classroom environment, e.g. lighting, heating, ventilation, displays, interior design
  o Development of spaces where students congregate or are in transit, e.g. halls, dining area, corridors, entrance areas
  o Development of school grounds, e.g. landscaping and habitats, litter, play areas, works of art, traffic and parking (cars and bikes)
  o Conservation and energy efficiency, e.g. water recycling, energy savings (solar panels, etc.), cleaning, information technology (IT) systems.

- Give each group a brief and the information about the resources and experts at their disposal.

Plenary (50 minutes)

- Each group makes a presentation of its recommendations, and other groups have an agreed amount of time to discuss their suggestions.
- Experts make their comments on the suggestions.
- Ask two or three students to give their views on whether students would be as happy in a new school that was not built on green principles.

Assessment/homework:
At the end of the plenary, ask students for examples of how their commitment to finding green solutions influenced their decisions. Check that all understand how values and attitudes influence decisions and solutions to problems.

Ask students to identify jobs in the building of the new school that are (1) green industries and (2) done to meet green requirements.

Notes for learning support assistant:
Provide support agreed with class teacher to identified students with additional needs and others as appropriate.

Extension ideas:

- Have a group look at community use of the new school and managing the impact of the new school on the local community
- Run the activity within 'Second Life'
- Identify the chain of jobs that are involved in building a new school.

Review notes: How well did the students engage with the exercise? What were their main learning points?

Career growth

My career narrative

In the 11–14 age group, it is important to focus on enabling the students to start the process of telling their stories in order to begin to construct their career narrative. The word 'career' here is used in its broadest sense to mean a pathway through life. It is important to remember that, although students in this age group have not yet had lots of experience that could be described as career related, many have been through a major period of transition from primary to secondary education. For some, this has meant leaving friends behind, travelling independently to a different area and meeting people from a wider range of backgrounds. Reflecting back on their experiences of transition is a very useful way of starting the storytelling process.

Storytelling can be done in a number of ways – through writing, visually (painting, collage, photographs, recorded using a digital camera) or verbally (through discussion or interviews). Often a variety of methods ensures wider engagement with the process. Many students will need a clear structure to help them to begin this process. A useful way of starting the process is to ask them to tell the story of their life in the final year of their primary education. Because this is something familiar, it is likely that many will find it easy and interesting, even if they disliked primary school.

Encouraging students to begin to tell their stories is useful for a number of reasons.

- If a story is about me, it cannot be right or wrong – everyone can do it.
- It builds confidence and self-esteem.
- Storytelling can help pupils to process experiences and thereby understand themselves and situations better.
- Looking back helps them to look forward. (If X happened last time, what might happen next time?).

It is also important to understand that storytelling can be therapeutic and, in this regard, needs to be handled carefully, particularly in relation to issues of disclosure. The story is always important for the teller, so it must not be minimised in any way. Sometimes a story will show that the individual student needs support in order to process his or her experiences, which may involve referring them to another professional.

MICHAEL

Michael had always found writing, in particular free flowing creative writing, very difficult at school. When everyone else wrote a full page, Michael would write only a few lines. One of his primary school teachers (Mrs A) had often commented on his lack of ability in this area, and although academically able in other areas (particularly in maths), Michael was one of the last people in his class to get his 'pen license', which allowed him to use a pen instead of a pencil for his written work. Michael often spoke of Mrs A both at home and at school and of the injustices he felt.

Early on in his first year at secondary school, Michael was asked by his form tutor to write about what he remembered most from his time at primary school. Michael was immediately very keen to write about his experiences with Mrs A. He wrote three and a half pages (a real achievement for him!) about how he felt, and he drew a picture of Mrs A. He handed the work in and was pleased that he had written such a lot. He felt he had never received a good mark for this kind of writing before whilst at primary school and was amazed when he got the work back. The work was full of positive notes from his tutor, such as 'that must have been really difficult for you'. She commented on his lovely picture and gave him a merit. Michael began to enjoy writing more, and his confidence grew. Perhaps most significantly, Mrs A was never mentioned again.

As well as telling their stories, students also need the opportunity to discuss them with others who are more knowledgeable than themselves (ZPD). This again needs to be done carefully, by posing questions such as the following:

- What made you choose to write about that?
- Why was it important to you?
- What made you choose those particular pictures?
- What does this tell you about yourself?

ZPD

Learning in the ZPD means focusing on what comes next. For pupils in this age group, this will include a consideration of a range of issues. In the early days, they are likely to focus on coping with the major change from primary to secondary education that most of them will have experienced. This can include everyday issues such as finding their way around a new school (which for most will be much bigger than their primary school), getting to know lots of new people (students and staff), making friends, coping with more homework and so forth.

As the years progress, most will face some important career-related decisions about subject choice; some will decide to follow a vocational route rather than an academic route. Effective CLD will give students the opportunity to explore a range of options in order to enable them to begin to think strategically about the future. This will mean thinking about the next steps in relation to a number of different options and evaluating them side by side.

A number of exercises could be effective in helping pupils to think strategically about their option choices. Here are some examples:

- Case studies (real and anonymised, or imaginary) of young people who made good/ bad option choices. Ask the students to say what was good/bad about how the people made their decisions.
- Ask students to interview people in the year above them about how they made their option choices. Discuss this in a small group, and ask the group to present their findings.
- Ask the students to research particular career areas, to decide on the most important school subjects for that particular sector and to rank the subjects in order of importance. Make sure that a range of sectors is covered, and ask the students to present their findings.
- Ask the students to research vocational courses on offer in the area, in order to be able to participate in a class debate. (This house believes that academic qualifications are more valuable than vocational ones.)

Any activity that is organised needs to include discussion time so that students process what they are learning. In addition, asking them to present their ideas is useful because in order to explain something they need to understand it. Clearly, all of this must be done in a supportive and encouraging learning environment.

Sample lesson plan for career growth

Lesson plan template career growth 11–14

Teaching group (year group or specific needs group)
11- to 12-year-olds thinking about their experiences at primary school

Date/duration
Autumn term

Title overview
What was primary school like for me?

Curriculum links and standards (e.g. PSHEE)

LOs
By the end of the session pupils will be able to:

1. Reflect on their experiences at primary school
2. Understand more about themselves.

Resources/materials
Magazines, glue, paper and coloured pens

Preparation:
None

Activities (with approximate timings):
Introduction

- A short explanation of story writing and how it can help us to understand ourselves better. Explanation of the task. (5 minutes)

- Ask the students to write some notes about their time at primary school under the following headings:

  o My life at primary school – ups and downs, things I liked and disliked
  o My friends
  o My teachers
  o My favourite things
  o My least favourite things. (5 minutes)

- Ask the students to make a visual representation (drawing, collage of cutouts from the magazines) of one of the points they have written about. Tell them that they will be asked to share this with the class or a small group. (20 minutes)

Main activities and methods and techniques used (includes information about differentiation/personalisation) (10 minutes)

- Students write under each of the headings
- Students make a visual representation (drawing/collage)
- Each student describes what he or she has done and why.

Plenary (5 minutes)

- Students are asked to write down one new thing they feel they have learned about themselves.

Assessment/homework: discuss the visual representation with others (parents/carers, teachers) and make notes.

Notes for learning support assistant: individual students may need help and support, e.g. with thinking about what they have learned about themselves.

Extension ideas: students are to think about some of the other aspects in the list.

Review notes: how well did the students engage with the activities? Were there any surprising findings?

Conclusion

In this chapter, we have examined CLD for 11- to 14-year-olds. In the next chapter, we focus on working with young people who are 14 to 16.

Chapter 5

CLD 14–16

Introduction

In this chapter, we explore the needs of 14- to 16-year-olds. Erikson (1950) characterises adolescence as the stage when young people develop either a strong sense of self, a feeling of independence and control, or remain unsure about themselves and the future. The tension between individual and collective identity is also apparent. At school, it feels important to fit in and be part of the crowd, but students also want to explore who they are and who they could possibly become.

Positive role models worthy of imitation are important, and they tend to be found from personal contact and relationships rather than from icons with unattainable lives. Students will pick up their career exploration habits from their role models, so an observant teacher will try to harness this phenomenon to create a climate where individuals are proactive in managing their careers.

This is an important time for young people to gain first-hand experience of working life through volunteering, work experience and part-time jobs.

Work shadowing, enterprise activities, business simulations and money management activities can also help students prepare for working life.

At this stage, students are developing their capacity for self-reflection, and many are making a realistic appraisal of their choices and opportunities. The beginnings of the formation of relatively stable, long-term occupational interests can also be a feature of their development that can be supported by well-designed CLD programmes. Although their understanding of their own capacities is becoming more realistic, unrealistic aspirations remain a problem for some.

CLD programmes can help to develop their reasoning about career progression. Their understandings are still largely one-dimensional at this stage based on faith in relatively simple matching processes and sequencing of events that they expect to fall into place. Learning at this stage, which focuses on how to respond to influencers and chance events ('happenstance' and serendipity), is particularly helpful. Students need help to understand the psychosocial as well as the physical and economic impacts of their choices.

Career resilience

In terms of career resilience, we can help these young people to develop in all of the settings where opportunities arise. The key phrase is 'trying it out', which leads to clearer, evidence-based understanding of themselves and their abilities and limitations, and about the opportunities that may be available to them. CLD can offer not only the spaces to 'try out' such as work experience and enterprise activities in school, but also spaces to reflect on other, out-of-school experiences and opportunities.

Work experience and part-time work

The purpose and benefits of including experience of the working world in the curriculum may be different to those of a part-time job. The purpose of a part-time job is likely also to have a different role to that of work experience to the young person; the part-time job is not necessarily anything to do with longer term career goals or learning – it is usually about earning money. Likewise, work experience brings in no money, but it is useful to try out something you might be interested in doing later in life and also offers broader insights into the world of work.

But are these distinctions really that clear? Can young people build up resilience in their part-time job that stands them in good stead in other experiences of the working world? Can work experience offer opportunities to 'try something' that leads to a part-time job, or even more?

Experiences of the working world may take a number of forms. A one- or two-week block of time in a real workplace has been a familiar event in many schools in the United Kingdom for some years. However, the purpose and benefits of this exercise have not always been clear. Some felt it was a good opportunity to explore a particular area of interest, others to add important elements to their CV and some an opportunity for learning about the working world more generally. In many cases, it could be a combination of all three, and in some, sadly none of these objectives were achieved.

Work simulations or enterprise experiences in the school setting also offer the learner the opportunity to try out roles and responsibilities and see the consequences of actions or decisions made. They can experience the importance of team work, creativity, leadership and reliability within the relatively safe setting of a school. However, they do not impose the rigour or discipline of a part-time job in relation to independent travel, punctuality, accountability or the real-life experience of working alongside adults as well as with other young people.

However, most schools could offer an opportunity to get the best of all worlds through either a school production or sports event. Apart from perhaps the travel element, this offers a wide variety of learning opportunities. Even here there may be occasions when travel outside the school could be incorporated into the experience, e.g. visiting and negotiating with sponsors.

We will now look in more detail at how a large school event could be organised and learning for all maximised.

EVENT: LARGE END-OF-YEAR MUSICAL PRODUCTION

This is 'real', not simulated. The event will happen, resources have to be spent and income generated. Adult members of staff and other partners (e.g. parents and governors) will work alongside the young people and help with the interview process. If managed well, it can be a real learning experience for all involved, and because it is 'in school', the learning elements can be monitored and effectively achieved. Depending upon the size of the year group or school, all or a proportion of the year group can take part.

The essential 'departments' could be as follows:

Costume – design and production
Scenery – design and production
Sound
Front of house (ticketing and sales)
Refreshments – sourcing, preparation, serving and sales
Marketing and publicity – posters, advertising, programmes and sponsorship
Photography – still and video
Retail – sale of programmes, photos and DVD of production
Finance – management of costs and income
Performance – some members of the year group may be performers along with students from other year groups. Their 'interview' will take the form of an audition.

Each department will need a manager in charge and a staff of either one or two others or a large group. The important thing is that no one is guaranteed a job, just like in the 'real world'. But each person can apply for as many jobs as he or she wants to, and clearly, the aim is to find each young person a role and responsibility that he or she can feel is valued and important. For each job, they have to complete an application form, and, if they seem to have the skills or qualities needed, they will be interviewed. The feedback from these interviews is as important as the job itself. Some will be very disappointed but will need to be clear about why they didn't get the job they wanted through feedback. They must demonstrate their skills and qualities through evidence, experience or testimony.

So, how is career resilience developed through such a project? In Chapter 1, we looked at how resilience can be considered in a number of ways. Higgins (1994:373) described how it can be recognised: 'The capacity to spring back, rebound, successfully adapt in the face of adversity.' By contrast, Coleman and Hagell (2007:14) take a more developmental approach and look at how resilience can be developed: 'Resilience develops through gradual exposure to difficulties at a manageable level of intensity.'

The example of the school production presents opportunities for resilience to be recognised by the young people themselves, but perhaps more importantly, it enables them to develop and nurture qualities of resilience. Helping young people to cope with disappointment, to understand what they can and cannot do in response, will help them to 'bounce back' throughout their lives.

The follow-up to such an enterprise may be through the extracurricular activities in school, or in the further development of these interests and skills in free time outside of school. Self-selected extracurricular activities can, of course, be challenging and offer opportunities for resilience to be fostered. However, they offer less scope to do something different. The singers sing, and the sporty people do sport. But what *else* could they do?

The local labour market, businesses and organisations

As someone involved in CLD, it is always good to consider how aware you are of the range of businesses and organisations that provide a living for people in your area. In other words, what do people do who live in the neighbourhood where you work? In areas of high unemployment, the coexistence of social pressures and the issues dealt with by pastoral support in the school will be very clear. In the same way, in areas where workers commute to high-pressure jobs in a 24/7 culture, the effects on their children in terms of behaviour and temperament may also be apparent. An opportunity to explore where people live and work can be very useful.

AN EXERCISE ON YOUR LOCAL LABOUR MARKET

List as many friends and family as you can who live in your area. On a map, mark where they live and work and note what they do. Does a pattern emerge?

By asking friends and family, you can find out if patterns of work in the area have changed over the past decade. Do more people travel out of the area to work or into it? Do more people work at home, even part of the time? Now consider how you can share this understanding with your students. One way is to ask them to do a similar exercise and to work alongside local businesses to explain the key issues for them. You could also invite local business leaders and key public service personnel to present some of the challenges that your local labour market faces.

In the United Kingdom, for some years it has been the pattern that young people around the age of 15 go into the workplace for a period of one or two weeks to take part in or shadow a role. This encourages them to take a step into the world of work. Whether this is done in a formal structure or more informally with family and friends, the key learning intentions need to be explicit:

1. To experience the difference in culture and expectation between school and work:
   a. Appearance
   b. Behaviour
   c. Attitude.

2. To reflect upon their own skills, qualities and interests within a work setting:
   a. Do I feel that I could fit in here?
   b. Do I have anything to offer this kind of environment?
   c. What will I need to learn or learn to do to compete in this kind of work setting?

3. To understand the structures of organisations, including their lines of responsibility and communication.
4. To make links between the learning in education and the knowledge and skills needed in the world of work.

Sample lesson plan for career resilience

Lesson plan template

Teaching group (year group or specific needs group)
Year 9 – age 14

Date/duration
Part of PSHEE programme
Length of time – 50 minutes

Title overview
The work I do
   This lesson explores the notion of work, identities within work and transferable skills developed through work in different settings.

Curriculum links and standards (e.g. PSHEE)

• Self-awareness as part of personal development in PSHEE, history, business studies, psychology, human geography, religious studies.

LOs
By the end of the lesson the students will:

1. Be able to describe at least three opportunities/contexts for work for me
2. Have listed the roles I play in different parts of my life
3. Have identified at least three skills or abilities that I have developed in one setting that I can use in others and in the future
4. Understand how adversity enables me to build resilience and strategies for managing difficult situations in the future.

Resources/materials

Preparation

Activities (with approximate timings):
Introduction/starter (10 minutes)

• Ask the group 'what is work?' List the answers given and, if needed, prompt discussion by asking, 'Is it still work if it isn't paid such as voluntary work or domestic caring?'
• Research shows that people earning lots of money (e.g. $100,000 per year) report that irrespective of how much they earn, they are no happier or content (Kahneman et al., 2006). So why else would people work, and work harder, if money is no longer the aim?

Main activities and methods and techniques used (includes information about differentiation/personalisation)

• In pairs, ask the group to discuss the roles and responsibilities they have at home/ community, at school and in paid work if they have any. What do they gain from each, apart from payment?
• These are collated in three groups: home/community, school and employment.
• Some students may need support and encouragement to identify some of their roles and responsibilities. If so the following examples could be used to prompt them:

Home/community	*School*	*Employment*
Taking out the rubbish (responsibility)	Class representative (reliability)	Babysitter (creativity and initiative)

- From these three roles, the individual gains these skills but also enjoys feelings of being valued, being recognised and being trusted. So they feel good about themselves. (25 minutes)
- The notion of resilience is explained as the ability to learn from and bounce back from adversity or difficult experiences, so without difficulties we cannot develop resilience. Some of these difficulties are encountered at work or during the process of education and career building. Explain how important these lessons and the building of such career resilience are in today's working world.
- Choose a story or example of someone your students would know about who has overcome adversity, put that experience to good use and built resilience. One example could be Bob Champion the jockey. The film *Champions* (1983) could be referred to or a clip shown. But anyone known to you or your students would be a good local example. (15 minutes)

Plenary

- Summarise what has been covered in this lesson – work is not just what we are paid for, and we gain a lot more from working experiences than just payment. We gain skills, self-esteem, identity and experiences. One of the most useful experiences is that of adversity or difficulty because we can use these to build the resilience we will need in our futures.

Assessment/homework:
Ask the students to write a paragraph about a difficulty they have overcome. 'How did it feel at the time and how do you feel about the way you responded to it?'

Notes for learning support assistant:
Support in the classroom may be needed to encourage discussion and to get contributions from all of the learners. Care will be needed also to ensure that there are no unchecked inappropriate comments about race/culture.

Extension ideas:
Make a list of roles and responsibilities that learners in this establishment can be given. How are they allocated? What skills are required and what are gained?

Review notes:
How well did the students link the notions of work, skills/abilities, adversity/difficulty and resilience?

Career happiness

Career happiness and citizenship education

Citizenship education has a key part to play in promoting understanding of career happiness with this age group. The draft Key Stage 4 Programme of Study in England (DfE, 2013), for example, encourages pupils to learn about the role of governments in helping people to enjoy their rights and how they can hold governments to account as active citizens. It also requires them to learn about the opportunities to participate in community volunteering.

Valuing happiness

THE PURSUIT OF HAPPINESS

Students help the Head of Year organise an Assembly for Independence Day on 4 July. One student describes how Americans celebrate Independence Day. Another student narrator talks about the significance of the celebration by saying that in 1776 Thomas Jefferson penned the famous phrase in the Declaration of Independence that people 'hold these truths to be self-evident, that all men are created equal, that they are endowed by their creator with certain unalienable Rights, that among these are Life, Liberty and the pursuit of Happiness'.

The Head of Year comments that these ideas are fundamental to the American way of life and this assembly is about the last of them – the pursuit of happiness. They explain that four students have been asked to talk about what the pursuit of happiness means to them. After they have spoken, some reflections are offered by the Head of Year on what they have said, including making these points:

- What did Thomas Jefferson mean by the pursuit of happiness? Did he mean happiness in the sense of having fun like Americans do on Independence Day? Or, more likely, was he really talking about something closer to the idea of being able to lead a life that goes well for you, that enables you to flourish and discover meaning and purpose in your life?
- Is there any good higher than the pursuit of happiness? Many people would argue that leading a good life is more important, and that you should rethink your happiness if it is based on behaving badly.

The assembly ends with a minute's silence to enable everyone to think how to pursue happiness well at home, in school and in their careers.

CHILD LABOUR

Ask the class if they have read any stories recently about the exploitation of child labour in the United Kingdom or abroad. One student mentions immigrant boys in a southern European city who make a precarious living by cleaning the windscreens of cars that are stopped at traffic lights. The class discuss why this kind of employment exists, who benefits from it and whether or not it should be stopped.

Explain that Article 4 of the United Nations Convention on the Rights of the Child (DfE, 2012), which applies to everyone up to the age of 18, states that governments must do all they can to make sure every child can enjoy their rights. One of these rights is protection from work that is dangerous or that might harm their health or education (Article 32). Ask students to think about how being able to live healthily and engage in learning can engender happiness.

Students go on to discuss how children may derive some kind of happiness from working for money or financial security. They realise that happiness is subjective and that the interplay of factors which contribute to personal happiness vary from individual to individual. Invite the students to think about the difficulties that governments and other regulatory bodies face in legislating in the area of children's work.

Put the students in groups of four to six, and give each group an issue to discuss. The issues are babysitting, Saturday jobs, paper rounds, working in the evenings after school, making and assembling things at home, working for your parents and making and selling things for charity. In their groups, students discuss:

- Who benefits from this type of work?
- What are the risks to children and young people who do this type of work?
- How would you regulate this type of work to protect the happiness and well-being of children and young people?

In the plenary discussion, provide information about legislation and local by-laws relating to child labour and where students can find out more about child protection.

Finding inner happiness

HAPPINESS AND CELEBRITY

'Happy. Free. Confused. Lonely. At the same time.' Read out this tweet by Taylor Swift, a bestselling female music artist. Students discuss the perils and payoffs of celebrity. This is a lead in to a topic on career success and celebrity to enable students to have a more realistic understanding of a career as a celebrity and apply the insights they gain to their own career planning, for example:

- Reality TV is sometimes seen as a short-cut to celebrity. Is there really any alternative to putting in the time and effort?
- How much resilience do celebrities need to cope with the stresses and pressures of fame?
- How easy is it to sustain a career as a celebrity without real talent, e.g. just by being famous for being famous?
- How easy is it to cope with the ups and downs of fame?

Ask the students to work in groups to create their own magazine articles about 'How to be a celebrity and stay happy'. Suggest that they could include the typical information found in career guides, for example:

- Where are the openings? (e.g. pop star, scientific celebrity, socialite . . .)
- What sort of person do you need to be?
- How do you get started?
- What are working conditions like?

- What are the prospects like in this role?
- What effect will it have on your lifestyle?
- What can you do if it doesn't work out? (e.g. have a job as a lookalike, work for a celebrity)

SERENDIPITY

Students hear how Newton, Nobel, and Pasteur all made discoveries as a result of serendipity or 'happy accidents'. Explain how people like scientists and detectives are trained to look for clues in their data or evidence that might lead to an unexpected breakthrough. Make the connection with what the students have been doing about career happiness so the students then consider whether 'career happiness favours the prepared mind'. (This is a deliberate misquote of Louis Pasteur's comment that 'Luck favours the prepared mind'.) They discuss how realistic it is to think that people's careers will unfold as a result of a simple careers plan and how 'chance' opportunities can impact on people's career happiness. Students realise that they need to know how to evaluate opportunities before selecting them and that they may still need to show adaptability and resilience if the opportunity does not turn out as expected!

Maximising happiness

CAREER HAPPINESS ON OFFER

Students take on the roles of advertising copywriters and create slogans and text for an advert for the Happiness Island Tourist Authority (HITA). HITA is looking for someone who is willing to give up his or her present job for a 'dream job' as tourist ambassador for Happiness Island. The person will live rent-free on the tropical island and receive an attractive salary. The job duties include exploring the island, protecting the wildlife and enjoying the outdoor sports and social life on the island. The person will write up his or her adventures in a weekly blog.

Students discuss the techniques they have used to sell the vacancy; home in on an important fallacy that advertisers exploit. Consumers are led to believe that happiness can be acquired or bought. People who strongly believe that the next move will make them happy experience more unhappiness in their present jobs. Tell students about 'habituation' which refers to people's capacity to become used to the status quo. People have a tendency to adjust or adapt to their circumstances – either good or bad. Much depends on their temperament, but an individual who changes jobs to secure their dream job will soon return to their own set point or baseline level of happiness. Even prisoners can come to feel that being in prison is not so bad after all.

Use the insights from this activity to explain why levels of happiness in society have remained relatively stable despite the overall increase in average wealth and why it is important not to make your happiness too dependent on meeting particular goals.

JUST DOING MY JOB*

Introduce the topic of job satisfaction with an extract from the story of Elmer Ruiz, a gravedigger, told to Studs Terkel who interviewed hundreds of people about their working lives. Elmer took pride in making a neat job of the graves he dug, and his skill was recognised by a sewer digger who came to see him once. He loved being outdoors, especially in the summer, but even in the winter, the time just seemed to rush by. Elmer never thought about his job at home because he loved listening to and playing music so much. He would have liked to have been a musician.

Students discuss Elmer's career happiness. From there, they go on to consider the following:

- A definition of job satisfaction (positive feelings about one's job).
- The connection between individual job satisfaction and career happiness.
- Why organisations might be interested in job satisfaction and career happiness (productivity, retention of staff, etc.).
- Which theories shed light on the causes of job satisfaction, e.g. career matching theory (Holland, 1973); Herzberg, Mausner and Snyderman's (1959) two-factor theory; Warr's (2007) theory of psychological 'vitamins'; the Hawthorne effect (Landsberger, 1958) and the mixed results when these ideas have been put to the test.

Arrange for the class to search for published stories in the media and on the Web that could be used to find out more about job satisfaction and to present their findings in a class blog. Students spend some time first brainstorming how to analyse people's stories. They also talk about getting an interesting cross section of people to interview (e.g. people from different sectors, at different stages in their careers, with a protected characteristic, with a different socio-economic status).

*This is the title of James Knight's collection of stories of cops, firies and ambos across Australia who, as the book jacket proclaims, 'have their own hardships to deal with but they still get up every day and make a difference'. It was published by Hodder Australia in 2006.

JOB SATISFACTION

Students take part in a business enterprise game. 'Duck production'* is a manufacturing simulation. Companies make paper ducks to order. They gain experience of basic accounting, organising production, meeting customers' needs and marketing. They also practise key skills such as communication, numeracy, problem-solving, teamwork and enterprise. The game lasts 60–90 minutes and requires basic equipment such as rulers, pencils, scissors, paper money and coloured A4 paper. Each 'day' in the game lasts 7 minutes.

Use the game to lead a structured discussion on job satisfaction to enable students to evaluate the work culture and environment of organisations to which they are thinking of applying. They will have an opportunity to do this next when they go out on work experience placements. Use these prompt questions:

- What did you enjoy about the job you have just been doing, and why?
- What bored or frustrated you, and why?
- Why are companies interested in improving job satisfaction for the people who work for them?
- What are the ways companies can increase job satisfaction for individuals and groups?
- Why is job satisfaction important for individuals?
- What would you include in a checklist of things to look out for if you are appraising a job opportunity?

*Johnson, Marks, Matthews and Pike (1987)

Lesson plan for career happiness

Teaching group

Date/duration
60 minutes

Title overview
Unemployment
    A session to help students understand ways of coping with being unemployed for a short while.

Curriculum links and standards

- 'Be positive about your own story and the responsibility you are taking for your own progress, achievement and well-being' (KS4 LO, *The ACEG Framework for Careers and Work-Related Education*; CDI, 2012:12).
- 'Show that you have acquired and developed qualities and skills to improve your employability' (KS4 LO, *The ACEG Framework for Careers and Work-Related Education*; CDI, 2012:13).
- Cross-curricular links: English, physical education (PE).

LOs
By the end of the session, students will be able to:

- Identify ways of staying positive, healthy and safe during a period of unemployment
- Identify opportunities while unemployed for gaining useful experience that will enhance their CVs.

Resources/materials

- Outside speakers
- Access to careers pages on school VLE with information on leisure opportunities, sources of advice including financial support.

Preparation:

Invite three to four youth members of the council's children's and young people's trust to talk about the opportunities and support available for young people facing a period of unemployment.

Activities (with approximate timings):

Introduction (10 minutes)

- What students will get from the session (see LOs).
- Brainstorm 'Why do young people become unemployed?' (e.g. poor attendance at school, family difficulties, personal problems, lack of opportunities).
- Brief introduction to the scale of youth unemployment locally and what different agencies are doing to tackle the problem.

Main activities (20 minutes)

- Introduce youth members of the children's and young people's trust who are going to give a short presentation on the support and opportunities available to help young people get through a period of unemployment.
- Divide students into discussion groups, and invite visitors to circulate around the groups. Give groups a discussion brief:

  o Identify five negative feelings that unemployed young people need to try and overcome.

  o What can young people do to overcome those negative feelings while they are unemployed?

  o How can unemployed young people still get experience of work that will stand them in good stead when they apply for paid jobs?

Plenary (30 minutes)

- Ask groups for feedback on the discussion questions. (Manage the time so that each issue is discussed, and make sure each group has a chance for feedback, e.g. ask for one suggestion from each group).

Assessment/homework:

Check that all students understand the meaning of the terms used to describe young people's feelings (e.g. alienation, exclusion, despair, rejection).

Notes for learning support assistant:

Provide support agreed with class teacher to identified students with additional needs and others as appropriate.

Extension ideas:

- Discuss the treatment of unemployment in plays (e.g. *Blood Brothers*), novels (e.g. *Of Mice and Men*), and poetry (e.g. 'The Times are Tidy' by Sylvia Plath and public poems on joblessness on the Web).

Review notes: What insights did the students gain in relation to issues faced by people who are unemployed? Is any follow up needed?

Career growth

My career narrative

Ideally, by the time students reach the age of 14 they will have become used to telling their story in a number of different situations, including their CLD activities. Of course, they may not necessarily identify it as such or give it this label, but they will be engaged in storytelling nonetheless. Previously in this chapter, the issue of work experience and part-time work was discussed, and this provides fruitful ground for building the career narrative through storytelling. This could be done in a number of ways, such as the following:

- Asking students to write a story of their work experience. These stories could be read to younger students in the school, published in an issue of the school magazine or placed on the school's website.
- Asking students to keep a diary of their time on work experience. This could be written or recorded (audio or video).
- Asking the students to interview one another to find out about the highs and lows of being on work experience. Students could then draw out the main points and make a visual representation of them (e.g. a collage, display).

In any such activity, it is important to ask the students to think about the following:

- What were they expecting from their time on work experience?
- Was it what they expected?
- What assumptions did they make beforehand?
- Were there any surprises?
- How did they feel about the whole experience?

These questions will help them to analyse their experience rather than simply describe it. This storytelling will then prompt them to think about the future.

A DIARY EXAMPLE

Sunday – so tomorrow's my first day at the chemist shop. I've been looking forward to this for ages, but now it's almost here I suppose I'm a bit scared. Hope I don't muck something up and get the sack even before I've started! What am I going to wear? They're going to give me a uniform; hope I don't look like an idiot. Guess that means I can wear what I like underneath.

Monday – got up early. Wanted to make sure I didn't oversleep, so asked my Mum to wake me up in good time. Had breakfast and went for the bus. Good job I allowed a lot of time, as the bus was late and I only just got there. Really nervous. Met the manager and the person I am going to be working with. Lots of talking and observing people today. Had lunch in the canteen. People seem OK but not many my age.

Feeling a bit better about what I've got to do. Wish my shoes were more comfortable – didn't realise how much time I'd spend on my feet.

Tuesday – slept in a bit late and missed the bus. Got to work five minutes late and the manager was cross. Embarrassing. Said I was really sorry that I would work a bit later to make up the time. Must make sure I am on time tomorrow. Filled some shelves this morning and felt like at least I was doing something useful. Afternoon was really quiet – a bit boring really. My friends popped in after school, but the supervisor didn't seem happy, so they left.

Wednesday – got up early and got there on time – phew! Supervisor showed me how to use the till today. Seemed easy, but when I had a go and she watched, I thought I was really slow. Really worried about making a mistake. She said I did OK and that it takes practice. Can I see myself working in a shop? Not sure yet. It was really quiet again this afternoon and the time really dragged. Asked to clean some shelves and at least that made the time go quicker. Not my idea of fun though.

Thursday – on time again. I'm getting the hang of this! Customer came and asked me about hairdryers this morning. I showed them all the different ones on display, and they asked me about what the difference was between them. Thought about asking my supervisor, but they were busy. So looked at them with the customer, and we worked a few things out. It was really good speaking with someone rather than just filling shelves or helping to pack bags. Felt useful, and I now know more about which hairdryer I want for my birthday!

Friday – last day. Quite sad really. Overall it's been good, especially when I got the hang of things. The people are nice, and I think that's what matters. It must be horrible if you don't like the people you work with. Feeling really tired though. Being on your feet a lot is hard, and you always have to be polite to people, even when they're in a bad mood. Do I still want to work in a shop – maybe. Need to think about what kind of shop though. And do I want this for the rest of my life?

ZPD

For many young people, this period is one where they begin to think about their next steps to becoming an older and more independent teenager. Their sense of self continues to develop, and they begin to imagine themselves in a range of different situations outside home and school. Throughout this time, they continue to question what is important for them, what they are good at and what they enjoy. Activities that help them to explore these issues in greater depth will be valuable in helping them to progress in their thinking about career.

Some possible examples are as follows:

- Ask the students to turn the clock forward by one year. Where will they be? What will they have achieved? How will they feel? They can then do the same activity for a friend, exchange what they have written and compare the two accounts. Where are the similarities? Where are the differences? What can they learn from this about themselves?
- Ask the students to work in pairs to research two contrasting education and training opportunities in their local area (one academic and one vocational). Ask them to

compare the two and to discuss their strengths and weaknesses and to prepare a short presentation describing the opportunities, saying which they would prefer and why.

- Ask the students to think about the person they most admire or a role model. This could be someone famous or someone they know personally. Ask them to do some research to find out what that person was doing when they were the same age as them. What choices did they face? What decisions did they make? How was it different for them? What factors did they have to take into account? What barriers did they face? How did they make progress towards their goals? Ask them to write a short reflective account to summarise what they have found. These could then be put together to form a display.

- Using the material from the previous activity, ask the students to think about life in the shoes of their role model. Ask them to write 'a day in the life of . . .' in the first person, thinking about their way forward from that point.

To make the most of all of these activities, it will be important to ensure that students have discussion time, in order to enable their thinking to move forward.

Sample lesson plan for career growth

Lesson plan template career growth 14–16

Teaching group (year group or specific needs group)
Any group within the 14–16 age range

Date/duration
At any point

Title overview
Turning the clock forward

Curriculum links and standards (e.g. PSHEE) Personal wellbeing in PSHEE, English.

LOs
By the end of the session students will be able to

1. Think about where they might be in one year's time
2. See some of their potential from a friend's perspective
3. Identify the similarities and differences between their own perspective and that of a friend.

Resources/materials
Paper and pens

Preparation:
None

Activities (with approximate timings):
Introduction

- A short explanation of the exercise – looking into the future. Explanation of the task. (5 minutes).

Main activities and methods and techniques used (includes information about differentiation/personalisation)

- Write the date on the board (today's date but one year ahead).
- Ask the students to write about themselves under the following headings:

    o   Where will they be?
    o   What will they have achieved?
    o   How will they feel? (5 minutes)

- Then ask them to do the same activity for a friend. (5 minutes)
- Exchange what they have written and compare the two accounts.
- Discuss this with their friend and think about the following:

    o   Where are the similarities?
    o   Where are the differences?
    o   What can they learn from this about themselves? (10 minutes)

- Summarise these points and share them with the class. (10 minutes)

Plenary (5 minutes)

- Ask students to write down one new thing they feel they have learned about themselves.

Assessment/homework: discuss the piece with others (parents/carers, teachers) and make notes.

Notes for learning support assistant: individual students may need help and support, e.g. with thinking about what they have learned about themselves.

Extension ideas: students are to think about some of the other aspects in the list.

Review notes: how well did the students engage with the activities? Were there any surprising findings?

Conclusion

In this chapter, we have examined CLD for 14- to 16-year-olds. In the next chapter, we focus on working with young people who are 16–19.

Chapter 6

CLD 16–19

Introduction

This chapter focuses on delivering effective CLD with students aged 16 to 19 years old. Young people at this stage are capable of understanding career as a dynamic process (Howard and Walsh, 2011). They can begin to use systems thinking (Patton and McMahon, 2006) to make sense of the complex interactions between self, role, relationships and situation in terms of career choice and progression. Well-designed careers programmes develop students' abilities to strengthen their career adaptability and resilience, solve problems and develop robust propositions relating to career happiness. They should be encouraged to take greater responsibility for their CLD by maintaining a careers portfolio, conducting researches and implementing their own action plans. They should have opportunities to discuss controversial matters in careers and work, including issues related to democracy and markets, corporate work cultures, equality, social justice and sustainable development.

Students should also prepare for making choices and decisions, as well as understanding the personal and financial consequences of their chosen pathways. This is also a good time to help them develop high-level job-seeking skills and to learn about negotiating transitions such as the move from school to an apprenticeship, job or further study.

Career resilience

For this group, the ongoing development of resilience is crucial before they enter further education or HE or the world of work. Many of the traditional tenets of school life such as the lessons of the sports field will by now either have been learnt or abandoned.

Earlier foci have shifted, and many young people will now have a fairly clear idea of the direction they would like to go in; some, however, will not. But even for those with a clear focus and interest, as in the case of Ruth in Chapter 1, the story is far from over. This is a time to look back over their school and home lives before looking forward – for thinking about how opportunities have come about, how choices have been made and how these have shaped the individuals and their views of themselves. Of course, this may be the last thing that they want to do. Being 16+ is about looking forward to the rest of your life, so how can we help young people to do that with confidence? In this section on building resilience, we revisit the three protective factors of I am, I have and I can (see Chapter 1). We focus on three examples of these, from factors first described by Coleman and Hendry (1999) as follows:

1. Problem solving (I am and I can)
2. Positive relationships and attachments (I have)
3. External interests and activities (I can and I have).

Problem solving through peer mentoring

Helping to solve the problems of others is a great way to develop problem-solving skills for yourself. Many schools have buddy or peer support schemes that help to develop interpersonal skills, responsibility and community spirit. However, there is also some career learning that can happen here. Through the process of supporting someone else, mentors have the opportunity to reflect on their previous, possibly similar experiences and how they have since grown and developed.

Smith, Howard and Harrington (2005:33) define a mentor as 'a more senior person who takes an interest in sponsorship of the career of a more junior person'. The goal of peer mentoring is the socialisation and, to some extent, the education of the mentee. 'Sponsoring' a younger student requires maturity and responsibility, characteristics that contribute to career growth as well as to CLD more generally.

Exploring positive relationships and attachments

Social networking sites may seem to encourage a competitive attitude to the number of friends we all have. Sometimes it might seem you are sad and lonely if you have less than 200 'friends'. However, for many of us the number of true friends and close family that we can really rely upon can be closer to 20 than 200. Friendship can be a risky business; when we trust someone and that trust is broken, it is a painful experience. So how do we nurture positive attachments yet remain resilient to the danger of disappointment and rejection? This will be a familiar problem to young people in this age group, some of whom are developing and recovering from romantic liaisons on a regular basis.

This is tricky territory; if asked to list the names of trusted friends and family, many may feel uncomfortable and vulnerable. The use of other people's stories, however, can help individuals to reflect on their own situation.

Case studies or well-known stories from soap operas or films can be useful. The film *The Incredible Journey* (1963) is an excellent illustration of this. In the film, three friends (animals) set out on a long and dangerous journey to find their family. Their characters, frustrations, and loyalties are tested, and ultimately, they succeed because of them.

Choose a story that is well known to your students and that will help them to think about their own relationships. Ask the students to consider the following questions:

* How are friendships founded? (e.g. common interests, shared values)
* What strengthens friendships? (e.g. adversity, trust)
* What threatens friendships? (e.g. familiarity, distance)

Ask the students to consider what it means to be popular.
Ask them to consider the following questions:

* Why does it matter so much what others think of us?
* What is more important – the number of 'friends' or the length of the friendship?
* Does our behaviour always reflect the important aspects of friendship?

What is it about friends and family you can rely upon that helps to build resilience? Could it also make them less self-reliant? Ask the students to list or discuss why they may be able to deal with problems or disappointments more easily if they have friends and family to back them up. What is it that these relationships give us?

External interests and activities

Interests outside day-to-day school or work life help to build resilience (Coleman and Hendry, 1999). This may be because it gives us a balanced perspective and a broader range of personal contacts, or because it spreads learning about the risks inherent in our everyday lives across a range of contexts. If all a young person does is go to school and come home again, their experience will be narrower than if they were also part of the wider community. Where they may not have had the opportunity to shine or excel in one context, they may be able to in another.

GRAHAM

Graham is 16 and attends a large school in a large town. He is an only child and close to both his parents. He is quiet and of average ability. He is rarely in the spotlight and has only a few good friends that he hangs out with at break times during the school day. Graham is slightly overweight and does not really enjoy football or athletics.

One morning he is called to attend his careers interview with the careers adviser. His records indicate an unremarkable, unfocused young man who may well need some help, if he is to find his direction in life. However, when the careers adviser asks Graham if he has any particular ideas or interests that he might like to pursue in the future, he states clearly and confidently that he has a golf handicap of three and that he will be leaving school at the end of the year to concentrate on becoming a professional player.

No one in the school, apart from his two friends (who had always thought he was making it up) had any idea about Graham's 'other life'.

This could go some way to explaining why Graham didn't get as annoyed as others when he wasn't chosen for the team or a part in a play or didn't get to dance with the most popular girl at discos.

However, we hear stories of children and young people who take part in a different activity every evening. Tennis on Monday, swimming on Tuesday, piano lessons on Wednesday and youth club on Thursday, leaving choir for Fridays and the weekends playing team sports and visiting friends. A balanced life is important because it allows time for interests and activities to be enjoyed.

Nonetheless, the skills and experiences gained from relationships and activities outside school and home can have a big impact on the ability of an individual to cope in unfamiliar surroundings, deal with change and address challenges.

LAUREN

Lauren is 17 and attends a small girls' school in a large city. She is a bright and confident student and is often called upon to sort out arguments between friends or to solve problems in their love lives. When the students are invited to take part in some community work in a local day centre for the elderly, Lauren is enthusiastic. Some of her friends complain that it will be boring, that they won't know what to talk to the service users about and dread the day that the project begins. However, Lauren immediately introduces herself to a group of older people and begins to chat away about all kinds of topics. Some of the other girls hang about in groups talking to each other; they look awkward and out of place. On the bus back to school later that day, she explains that she's been part of a community choir since she was 7, which has men and women of all ages in it as well as children. So even though she doesn't have grandparents living nearby, she's quite used to talking to older people.

How might this confidence and ability help Lauren in her future education and career?

Lesson plan on career resilience

Lesson plan template

Teaching group (year group or specific needs group)
P16

Date/duration
September/50 minutes

Title overview
Learning through adversity

Curriculum links and standards (e.g. PSHEE)
PSHEE, history, human geography, religious studies.

LOs
By the end of the lesson the learners will:

1. Be able to explain why mistakes and failure are important
2. Have identified three examples in their own life when they have learnt through adversity
3. Have recognised the development of resilience through dealing with adversity in a well-known person
4. Understand how to maximise learning in these opportunities.

Resources/materials

Preparation:
YouTube clip of someone on a trampoline
Power ball.

Activities (with approximate timings):
Introduction/starter (5 minutes)

- Using a power ball, the teacher demonstrates how the harder it is thrown to the floor, the higher it bounces. The class are asked why this happens. The answer is that energy in one direction is stored and released in the opposite direction. Someone bouncing on a trampoline is another example – a short clip of this could be shown if possible.

Explain that this session is about how the energy and learning of what might be thought of as mistakes, failures or even disasters can be stored and used for their benefit. But first they have to be recognised and learnt from.

Main activities, methods and techniques used (includes information about differentiation/personalisation)

- Students are asked to move into pairs and to list at least three occasions each when things have gone wrong. Give some examples such as losing a game of tennis, missing out to a more experienced candidate in a job interview and so forth. (15 minutes)
- Before sharing these, tell the story of King Robert the Bruce of Scotland.

Bruce and the spider

There was once a king of Scotland whose name was Robert Bruce. He needed to be both brave and wise, for the times in which he lived were wild and rough. The King of England was at war with him and had led a great army into Scotland to drive him out of the land.

Battle after battle had been fought. Six times had Bruce led his little army against his foes, and six times had his men been beaten and driven back. At last his army was scattered, and he was forced to hide himself in the woods and in lonely places among the mountains.

One rainy day, Bruce lay on the ground under an old shed, listening to the patter of the drops on the roof above him. He was tired and sick at heart and ready to give up all hope. It seemed to him that there was no use for him to try to do anything more.

As he laid thinking, he saw a spider over his head, making ready to weave her web. He watched her as she toiled slowly and with great care. Six times she tried to throw her frail thread from one beam to another, and six times it fell short.

'Poor thing!' said Bruce. 'You, too, know what it is to fail.'

But the spider did not lose hope with the sixth failure. With still more care, she made ready to try for the seventh time. Bruce almost forgot his own troubles as he watched her swing herself out upon the slender line. Would she fail again? No! The thread was carried safely to the beam and fastened there.

'I, too, will try a seventh time!' cried Bruce.

He got up and called his men together. He told them of his plans and sent them out with messages of cheer to his disheartened people. Soon there was an army of brave Scotsmen around him. Another battle was fought, and the King of England was glad to go back into his own country.

I have heard it said that, after that day, no one by the name of Bruce would ever hurt a spider. The lesson which the little creature had taught the king was never forgotten.

- What is the word used to describe this – tenacity/perseverance/resilience? Sometimes, like in this story, it is important to just keep trying. Are any of the examples from the students like this? (These could be about learning a new skill or sport, or about not giving up when there is still an opportunity to succeed.)
- But at other times, failure or adversity means we need to learn something about ourselves or about the decisions we have made. Are there any examples like this? (These could be when the adversity can be linked to something the individual has done, not done or could learn to do better such as interview skills, revision for an exam or modifying behaviours.)
- Invite the students to feed back their own examples, explaining which of these two categories they fit into. (20 minutes)

Plenary (10 minutes)

- Summarise what has been covered in this lesson – it is important not to ignore the lessons we can learn from adversity. Show a film clip or tell the story and show a picture of a well-known person who has achieved this. This could include people such as Bob Champion and Nelson Mandela or a well-known figure from the world of business, film or music.

Assessment/homework:
Taking one of your examples shared in class today, think of a motto or saying that would illustrate what this has taught you.

Notes for learning support assistant:
Support in the classroom may be needed to encourage discussion and to get contributions from all of the students. Care will be needed also to ensure that there are no unchecked inappropriate comments about race/culture.

Extension ideas:
Explore the story of the well-known person in the plenary, finding out more about how he or she turned adversity into success. Who helped the well-known person?

Review notes:
How well can these learnt attitudes and values be reinforced in other parts of the curriculum?

Career happiness

Valuing career happiness

SURVEYING HAPPINESS

Ask students the following three questions:

- What makes people happy at work?
- How happy are people at work?
- What would make people happier?

Now find out what they can learn about happiness at work from surveys and discuss why they should treat happiness surveys with caution, especially if they intend to let the results of surveys influence their thinking about their own happiness.

Give students the opportunity to look at the questions, methodology and results of a number of happiness surveys:

- Gallup-Healthways Well-Being Index (USA) (http://www.well-beingindex.com/default.asp)
- Measuring National Well-Being – Children's Well-Being 2013 (http://www.ons.gov.uk/ons/dcp171766_304416.pdf)
- The Oxford Happiness Questionnaire (http://happiness-survey.com/survey/)
- Happiness Works Survey (http://www.happinessatworksurvey.com/)

Afterwards, the students discuss some of the difficulties of designing happiness questionnaires and why people should interpret the results of surveys carefully, for example:

- Do not assume that in a survey you are discovering people's deep-seated values when you might just be finding out something much more superficial, e.g. how people feel in the present circumstances.
- Do not assume that everyone understands the survey questions in the same way.
- Bear in mind the principle of diminishing marginal utility. People value highly that of which they have little, i.e. those who are working long hours in high-income jobs are likely to favour some leisure above more work. However, those who are in low-income or part-time jobs are likely to have enough of leisure, preferring some more work. The principle applies to marginal preferences and not to people's underlying attitudes. It is only the preference for more leisure that increases when leisure decreases; the attitude towards leisure in general is not affected.
- Do not assume that people's behaviour correlates with their values, e.g. someone can say that they value leisure the most while working the long hours that go with their high-paid job.
- When people consider the impact of a single factor on their well-being (e.g. if they had more money), they tend to exaggerate its importance. Kahneman et al. (2006) call this 'the focusing illusion'. This can result in them over-predicting the gain in happiness if they concentrate on that factor (e.g. seeking higher income).

Finding inner career happiness

CAREER HAPPINESS AND SPIRITUAL WELL-BEING

The opportunity to reflect on the connection between spiritual well-being and lasting career happiness can be very helpful. This can be facilitated in a way that accommodates students with or without religious affiliation, at different stages of spiritual development and with different spiritual problem-solving styles.

Ask students to discuss the following questions:

- Do you think that work has meaning and purpose in people's lives? If your answer is 'yes' or a qualified 'yes', what is a good meaning and purpose?
- As well as becoming more aware of its meaning and purpose, what can people do to flourish at work and in their careers?
- How can you deepen your understanding of the meaning and purpose of work in your own life?
- What sources of inspiration have you found useful in deepening your understanding of the work you want to do in your own life?

Students make the link between work and personal identity – that work for some is just a job, while for others it may be a calling. They recognise that some people gain more fulfilment from their personal work than from their paid employment. Some students recall their sense of wonder and joy when they discovered a job that they really wanted to do. When students talk about 'good work', they mention doing work that is worthwhile, that contributes to the well-being of others and that fosters interdependence and supportive relationships.

Some mention life-work balance and living and working in harmony with the environment. They discuss whether materialistic attitudes foster fulfilment.

The students talk about being at ease and happy with themselves when they make time for reflection and contemplation. Some students know about techniques for relaxation and meditation. One student mentions groups of people in China and other countries who practise t'ai chi in public spaces before going to work to improve their health and well-being.

The following wisdom is shared and discussed:

- 'The miracle is not that we do this work, but that we are happy to do it.' (Mother Teresa)
- 'He who wants to do good knocks at the gate; he who loves finds the gate open.' (Tagore)
- 'The trouble with the rat race is that even if you win, you're still a rat.' (attributed to Lily Tomlin)
- 'A musician must make his music, an artist must paint, a poet must write if he is to ultimately be at peace with himself.' (Maslow, 1954)
- 'Your work is to discover your work and then with all your heart to give yourself to it.' (Buddha)

Signature strengths*

Twenty-four character strengths that a person might have are described, such as honesty, loyalty and wisdom. Students try to identify the top five signature strengths of famous literary, scientific and political figures and show how they used those strengths to overcome challenges.

The source of these character strengths (the free values-in-action [VIA] signature strengths questionnaire for 8- to 17-year-olds at http://www.authentichappiness.org) is explained. Students answer a bank of 198 questions online and receive a profile report showing their highest or signature strengths. They use their report to do the following:

- Discuss how they could enhance their happiness and well-being by using their top signature strengths as much as possible in school, in the workplace and with family and friends.
- Decide how they would write about their signature strengths in a personal statement.

*This exercise is adapted from an activity developed for the Positive Education project at http://www. authentichappiness.org.

Maximising happiness

CHAOTIC CAREERS

Chaos theory can appear to undermine the value of the career planning that students are asked to do. If only some of the predictions about the rapidly changing world of work are true, young people still have to prepare for unpredictable events that could change the trajectories of their careers. But how can this be done well? Adult self-help books suggest strategies for 'thriving on chaos', but which approaches could be relevant and appropriate for teenagers?

A series of activities can be developed to make ideas about chaos accessible, for example:

- Career patterns are often non-linear.
- Small causes can have big change effects.
- People can understand better what is happening to them if they use systems thinking to understand their careers.
- Complexity and change in the world of work casts doubt on the efficacy of simple matching approaches.
- Understanding the 'attractors' that influence behaviour can make a certain amount of prediction possible.
- We need to be realistic about what can be achieved in a single careers interview with an adviser.

Using anonymised case studies of students can help to raise awareness of the resources and skills that students can use to cope with the disorientation and stress of the seemingly random events that may befall them.

These case studies can be discussed to enable students to appreciate the following:

- Narrative approaches help individuals to accommodate chance events in their life stories and to understand their stories a little better (if not completely).
- Learned optimism can help individuals to respond creatively to chaotic events and discover new meaning in their work and lives.

- Habituation is a psychological response that 'kicks in' and helps individuals to return to their baseline level of happiness on which they can build.
- Individuals who suffer severe traumas may need specialist therapy to help their recovery.

Happiness and the work ethic

The combination of factors that make up happiness for each individual is unique. Empirical studies show that lack of job satisfaction and alienation from work produce feelings of unhappiness. A route to happiness based on developing a positive work ethic can be found. This can be defined as individuals being intrinsically motivated to do a 'good job', for example, by choosing work that is meaningful and worthwhile.

Max Weber's concept of the 'Protestant work ethic' is discussed and its origins traced back to the Old Testament story of work as a punishment for Adam and Eve's transgression. Students look at evidence of its continuing importance from a recent study that found that individuals in Protestant societies are more adversely affected by unemployment than others (van Hoorn and Maseland, 2013). The teacher argues that a virtuous work ethic need not be a joyless pursuit, but rather one in which individuals derive pleasure from doing work that is creative, purposeful, fulfilling and contributes to the well-being of others.

Good work

Students examine the proposition that 'happiness is doing good work'. They consider the following:

- The nature of good work, e.g. is 'good work' work done well, and/or is it work that contributes to the well-being of society as well as to the well-being of the individual? Can you do good work in every sector of the economy or just in those that meet certain values such as ecological living and caring for people?
- The relationship between doing good work and feeling good – can doing good work make you feel unhappy and vice versa?
- The importance of meaning in life – is feeling good more about deriving a sense of purpose in life rather than happiness?

Organise a 'fishbowl' to discuss 'How much responsibility do people have for doing good work?' Ask four teachers from different areas of the curriculum – business studies, religious studies citizenship and psychology – to debate the issue in front of the students. The teachers sit in an inner circle with the audience sitting in an outer circle around them. A fifth chair is provided in the inner circle for any student from the audience who wants to ask a question or join in the discussion briefly before returning to the outer circle to make way for another contribution from the audience. A lively debate can ensue about such things as unequal power relationships at work, whistle-blowing, economic pressures on organisations and perverse reward systems.

Volunteering

The school organises a wide range of opportunities for sixth formers to contribute to the well-being of others in the school and the local community. The vertical tutoring system gives students the opportunity to be positive role models for younger students. On one afternoon a week, sixth formers participate in community service projects in the local community. These projects range from running activities for children with special needs to visiting elderly people in local residential and day centres.

Through their participation in these activities, students learn that doing things for others increases reciprocal happiness and well-being. They discover the importance of offering and receiving gratitude. For some students, community service is initially just a way of improving their CVs, but they come to realise the value of 'gift work' and find out that they can continue to be involved through gap year charities, university schemes, and local organisations after they leave school.

Lesson plan on career happiness

Teaching group

Date/ duration
60 minutes

Title overview
Top ten
    Students critique the excellence, ethics and engagement (3Es) concept of 'good work' and identify ten individuals who exemplify good work in action. They reflect on the work values that are important to them in their careers.

Curriculum links and standards

- 'Recognise the personal, social and economic value of different kinds of work and be critically aware of key debates about the future of work' (P16 LO5, *The ACEG Framework for Careers and Work-Related Education*; CDI, 2012:14).
- Cross-curricular links: citizenship, religious studies.

LOs
By the end of the session, students will be able to:

- Critique the concept that 'good work' is excellent in quality, ethical and personally engaging (the 3Es)
- Explain the importance of good work to the happiness and well-being of individuals, organisations/professions and society
- Explain the challenges of carrying out good work
- Explain how they will give meaning to their work.

Resources/materials
The lesson is adapted from ideas and resources in *The Good Project Good Work Toolkit* (http://www.thegoodproject.org/pdf/GoodWork-Toolkit-guide.pdf).

Preparation

Activities (with approximate timings):
Introduction (15 minutes)

- Outline the objectives of the lesson.
- Read the verses attributed to Mother Theresa. Discuss the idea that having a calling involves a transcendental sense of purpose.
- Ask students how they define 'good work'. Introduce the 3Es concept from the Good Work project.

Main activities (30 minutes)

- In small groups of three to five, students record their ideas about what excellence, ethics and engagement mean in relation to 'good work'.
- Take feedback from each group and allow time for discussion of interesting points raised.
- In the same groups, ask students to choose a particular field (e.g. sport, science, the armed forces) and come up with their all-time list of top ten people in that field who did or do good work. The individuals chosen do not have to be famous.
- Groups explain their choices using the 3Es framework. Ask students about the causes of particular difficulties that any of these individuals faced in trying to do good work and what is known about how they feel about their work.

Plenary (15 minutes)

- Ask a student to explain the 3Es and how they contribute to career happiness and well-being.
- Give students two minutes to write a private reflection on doing good work and its meaning for the next stage of their career planning.

Assessment/homework:

- To discuss the 3Es with people at home.

Notes for learning support assistant:
Provide support agreed with class teacher to identified students with additional needs and others as appropriate.

Extension ideas:
Students investigate work cultures and issues such as corporate social responsibility.

Review notes: Ask students how they have developed their ideas about good work and happiness as a result of the session.

Career growth

My career narrative

In order to achieve career growth, students need opportunities to continue to articulate their career narrative. It is important to emphasise that by the time students reach this age they will have already made some career-related decisions, e.g. which subjects to study, whether to choose an academic or a vocational course, whether to stay in the same school or college or to move to somewhere different. These experiences can provide some of the fertile ground needed for their continuing career growth.

Helping students to tell their story can be done in a number of ways, and it is important to encourage them to do this in whichever way suits them best. Traditional methods would probably suggest that stories are usually told either verbally or through writing. Both techniques are undoubtedly valuable, and many students will gain a lot from an opportunity to discuss their experiences with others, particularly one-to-one. Writing involves a slower mental process than speaking, so often greater depth of thought is prompted through writing. However, storytelling should not be restricted to these two methods as many students learn in different ways. For example, Ruth (in Chapter 1) may well find it easier to think through her past experiences and tell her story by using visual methods (e.g. by putting together a career portfolio containing pictures, diagrams and articles cut out from magazines). Others may find compiling a playlist of their favourite music helpful, whilst others could use a digital camera to record their thoughts about their experiences.

Whichever method is chosen for the activity of storytelling, it is important to understand that on its own, this is not enough. To gain most from it, students will also need an opportunity to discuss the activity with someone. For example, Ruth would undoubtedly gain a lot from the activity of putting together her career portfolio, but explaining what she chose to include and why would certainly help her to gain a greater understanding of herself and what is important to her in relation to career. Through discussion of the relevant storytelling activity, new knowledge about career is constructed and career growth takes place, even if this appears as small steps forward or, in some cases, even steps that on the surface appear to be steps backwards. Helping students to tell their story and to process their previous experiences will enable them to continue to look to the future.

ZPD

Focusing on the next steps in their development will provide some of the impetus required for career growth. During this period, many young people have to consider the next big step forward as they reach the end of their school life; some will see this as the first potentially life-changing decision they have had to make. Some will be considering some form of HE at university or college, whilst others will be thinking about work, possibly in the form of apprenticeships, traineeships, internships or junior positions with employers. Whatever the context, for many young people this will be a stressful time where they feel the pressure of impending final examinations and coursework alongside the perceived need (e.g. from parents and teachers) for greater clarity about the future.

With such a lot at stake, focusing on the next steps can be helpful in reducing stress and enabling young people to make some progress in their thinking about career. Activities that help students to think in more depth about the decisions they will have to make from a range of angles will be helpful.

MY NEXT STEPS

Giving students case studies of young people's experiences at university can help them to think through a number of relevant issues which could influence their university choice and help them find out more about university life. These case studies can be real (e.g. previous students from the school or college which must be anonymised) or imaginary. Ask the students to discuss them and bring out the key points. These could include such things as feeling homesick, running out of money, feeling like they have chosen the wrong course, leaving a boyfriend/girlfriend behind at home, pressure from parents to do well, not getting on with people in their student accommodation and not realising they had to hand in work at a particular time as they hadn't attended lectures. The case studies themselves could be written, pictorial (e.g. from Google Images) or recorded and watched on screen. Students themselves can formulate the case studies by recording interviews with former students or writing about the interviews afterwards or carrying out research on YouTube to find useful clips.

Lesson plan template career growth 16–18

Teaching Group (year group or specific needs group)
16 to 17 year olds considering applying to college or university

Date/duration
Autumn term

Title overview
What do I need to think about when choosing where I want to study?

Curriculum links and standards (e.g. PSHEE)
'Research and evaluate progression pathways and return on investment for the higher and further education, training, apprenticeship, employment and volunteering options that are open to you' (P16, L014, *The ACEG Framework for Careers and Work-Related Education;* CDI, 2012:15).

LOs
By the end of the session students will be able to:

1. Understand more about the importance of university/college choice
2. Understand some of the pitfalls that could be avoided
3. Understand a range of issues that students face in their university studies.

Resources/materials
No specific resources required.

Preparation:
Prior to the session, students (working in pairs) will have been asked to find their favourite and least favourite clips about studying at university on YouTube. Ask them to come to the session prepared to show the clip and to say what they like/dislike about the clips.

Activities (with approximate timings):
Introduction and overview of LOs (5 minutes)

- Students are to think about a decision they have made recently – what went well and was there anything that could have been avoided? Discuss with a partner. Short feedback to bring out key points.

Main activities and methods and techniques used (includes information about differentiation/personalisation)

- Students show their clips and say what they like/dislike about them, what was useful/ not useful. (10 minutes per pair of students)
- The group decides which was the most useful overall and why, least useful overall and why. (10 minutes)
- What factors do I now want to take into account when thinking about where I want to study? Discuss in pairs and provide feedback to the group. (10 minutes)
- Individually, each student ranks the factors according to how important the issue is for him or her (personalisation). (5 minutes)

Plenary (5 minutes)

- Each student shares the factor that he or she ranked as number one.

Assessment/homework: discuss the factors with others (parents/carers, teachers and peers) and make notes.

Notes for learning support assistant: individual students may need help and support, e.g. with ranking choices.

Extension ideas: students are to think about how their ideas are changing and write some comments on this for the next session.

Review notes: how well did the students engage with the activities? Were there any surprising findings?

Conclusion

In this chapter, we have focused on CLD with young people aged 16–19, which concludes Part II. In Part III, we move on to examine a range of issues related to the leadership and management of CLD.

Part III

Developing your expertise in CLD

Chapter 7

Leading and managing CLD

Introduction

In Part I, we discussed how to construct a curriculum for CLD based on an effective peda-gogy and a commitment to principles and values that can make a real difference to young people's lives. In Part II, we illustrated this approach with lesson ideas and plans that will help schools to achieve worthwhile outcomes for their students. Throughout, we have addressed the reader as a career development professional. In Part III, we suggest ways that career development professionals can develop their expertise in CLD as a leader and manager. We discuss the issue of developing your role in relation to others and the benefits of formulat-ing a policy and development plan to drive the school's approach to its CLD provision. The chapter also looks at how to observe CLD sessions, facilitate the learning of colleagues, use records effectively and become a skilled CLD communicator.

Developing role clarity and clear role relationships

It is important to keep your job description up to date and to map your role in relation to other roles in leading and delivering the school's CLD provision. A template for carrying out an audit is presented in Table 7.1.

The role of the careers lead team

We use the generic term 'leader of CLD' partly in response to the current focus on leadership in the English school system but also because of the vastly different titles that exist in schools, e.g. Careers Coordinator, Head of Careers, Progression Manager. We also recognise that the leader for CLD could come from any professional background and be at any level in the management system of the school. The leader of CLD could be, for example:

- A senior school manager/leader
- A middle manager who is a teacher, a member of teaching support, a member of the administrative staff, a career development professional or an education-business links adviser who previously worked in industry
- A first-in-line manager from any of the backgrounds mentioned previously.

Table 7.1 Audit template

Key functional areas	Who does this in your school? (Tick as appropriate: √√ = has main responsibility √ = has some responsibility.)						
Clarify the scope and purpose of CLD	**SM**	**CL**	**SCS**	**ESC**	**SD**	**T**	**O**
Identify the CLD needs of students							
Identify how CLD in the curriculum can contribute to school effectiveness and improvement							
Manage CLD in the curriculum to meet identified needs							
Provide leadership and coordination of CLD							
Establish aims, objectives and intended outcomes							
Produce schemes of work and lesson plans							
Create, choose and organise a range of digital and other resources to support CLD							
Manage communications with students, parents/carers, staff and other key stakeholders							
Organise professional learning and development for staff							
Manage contracts and partnerships with external providers of services and support							
Assure quality and evaluate the effectiveness of CLD							
Deliver careers information							
Facilitate students' use of information to promote CLD							
Deliver careers education							
Facilitate CLD using a range of teaching and learning approaches							
Deliver career guidance							
Facilitate CLD using a range of helping and support strategies							

Key

SM = senior leaders and governors
CL = Curriculum leader for CLD
SCS = School careers specialist(s)

ESC = External careers specialist(s)
SD = subject staff in departments
T = tutors
O = other roles

It is for the school to determine the best leadership arrangements for CLD that will meet its needs. These are the main caveats:

- Experience suggests that a loose collective responsibility for CLD where everyone is responsible so often ends up as no one taking responsibility for making things happen.
- Leadership of CLD is not an isolated responsibility. Senior school leaders have overall responsibility for strategy, vision, quality and resources. Middle and first leaders have responsibility for curriculum and operational management issues, but responsibility for CLD is also a distributed leadership issue. CLD is the collective responsibility of all staff. All staff need to be involved in the change they want to see in their students.

As the lead for CLD, one of the most effective ways of getting the support you need is to set up a careers lead team. The exact membership will vary according to the needs of the school but could include the following:

- A senior leader who chairs the Careers Lead Team and ensures the vision and strategic leadership for the school's CLD provision.
- A 'Link' governor who will help to ensure that the school complies with its statutory obligations and meets community expectations with regard to CLD. A link governor can also help to mobilise resources in the community for CLD.
- A coordinator who is the school's main specialist careers professional and who is responsible for the direction and the day-to-day leadership and management of the CLD provision.
- Careers adviser(s) who deliver individual and small-group guidance as well as a range of support activities, e.g. up to date knowledge of the labour market.
- Careers administrator(s) whose role may include the following:
  o Maintaining the school's careers resource centre
  o Organising students' career guidance interviews and group work, online and face to face
  o Setting up and maintaining employer links and assisting in the placement procedures for work experience and volunteering.
- Student representatives who can contribute to the design, delivery and evaluation of the programme.
- Specialist staff who work in closely linked areas, e.g. the Special Educational Needs Coordinator or SENCO (learning difficulties and disabilities), PSHE coordinator (personal and social development).
- Staff representatives who can provide links into other groups of staff such as subject and tutor teams that are involved in the delivery of particular aspects of the programme.
- Community partners, e.g. parent representatives, local employers, local education providers.

The advantages of a careers lead team approach are that it:

- Enables staff to test the idea that teamwork supports career happiness and resilience
- Connects the work in careers to the overall leadership and performance of the school
- Encourages a proactive approach to the leadership, management and delivery of CLD

- Ensures that the school's response to the challenges of providing outstanding CLD is of sufficient magnitude
- Actively engages all relevant contractors, partners and stakeholders.

Before setting up or reviving a team approach, the school needs to do the following:

- Decide the composition of the team (it may be desirable to identify a core team and a wider team and have differentiated agendas to spare the wider team from sitting through lengthy meetings)
- Decide the frequency of meetings
- Agree a brief for the team and communicate it to all staff
- Agree a work plan for the year and provide written agendas and notes of meetings (forum software is ideal for managing this).

Developing policy

Every school needs a written policy for CLD to show the extent of its ambition to inspire young people about their future prospects, help them to make progress and achieve and meet their career development needs. A policy statement also shows how a school intends to fulfil its statutory obligations and to meet the wider expectations of parents/carers, employers and other community partners. The additional return on investment for the lead for CLD and the CLD team is that having a policy helps to accomplish the following:

- Establish consensus about what the school should be doing in a potentially contested area of school life
- Promote whole-school awareness of the importance of CLD
- Inform strategy and planning and give direction and purpose to the work of the lead for CLD and the team.

The school may choose to have either a separate policy document for CLD or a combined policy document for personal and social development. A combined policy document typically would cover the related areas of careers, work and economic life; family and friends; citizenship and community; personal growth and health.

To ensure that the policy for CLD is understood and agreed, it is helpful to develop it in consultation with those responsible for planning, delivering and reviewing provision, including young people themselves.

Although many schools will have a preferred format and style for their policy statements, the following is a useful structure for a policy document:

- Title
- Introduction (giving the background and context of the policy, what CLD is for, the school's commitment to this area, its relationship to other policies and how the policy was developed)
- Expected outcomes (what goals the policy is intended to achieve)
- Implementation (clarification of roles and responsibilities for leadership, management and delivery; an overview of the CLD curriculum and assessment)
- Partnerships (key stakeholders and providers with whom the school will work to achieve its policy goals)

- Budget and resources (the process of funding this area of the curriculum)
- Staff development (how the needs of staff responsible for CLD will be met within a reasonable period of time)
- Monitoring, review and evaluation (how the success of the policy will be judged)
- Approvals (signatures of head teacher and chair of governors, date of adoption, date of next review).

Setting development goals

Closely connected to policy is the CLD development plan. The development plan sets out the goals for the current year. As the development plan refers to new goals over and above the maintenance of existing activities, it is important to be realistic about what else can be achieved. The headings of the development plan will help to ensure this. For each goal, the plan needs to make the following clear:

- Who will lead the achievement of that goal
- The resources and support available
- The date for achieving the goal
- The success criteria.

Your development as a leader of CLD

One of the characteristics of a self-improving school system is that professionals must take greater responsibility for organising their professional learning and development from within their own institutions. As leader of CLD, this means taking responsibility for the following:

- Drawing up an annual personal and professional learning and development plan taking into account any recommendations from your professional association about making a commitment to continuing professional development. Remember that it is important to focus not only on the needs you have identified but also on the needs the school has identified, e.g. if you need to undertake professional learning to ensure that CLD can contribute to the achievement of specific goals in the school development plan. Listing your 'strengths', 'needs', 'opportunities' and 'barriers' will help you to set your goals.
- Keeping a professional learning portfolio or record. Include your action plans, details of participation in events, certificates awarded, thank you notes received (positive affirmations help to build your own career resilience and happiness) and reflections on experience (e.g. doing a critical incident review, keeping an achievements log).
- Using the feedback from appraisal to identify your next professional learning goals. As well as support from your line manager, it is worth considering a mentoring or peer-mentoring arrangement to help you reflect on your practice.
- Recognising that you learn in many different ways and not just through formal training, e.g. co-learning with your students, learning from the classroom resources you use to teach CLD, chatting with colleagues, working towards a quality award, doing work experience with a local employer.
- Getting involved in or helping to set up a professional learning community in your school or in a network of local schools.
- Joining a professional association such as the CDI (for practitioners in the United Kingdom).

- Undertaking professional learning in areas of educational management and leadership (e.g. project management, time management, managing communication, making presentations) as well as in CLD itself.
- Considering gaining a relevant accredited qualification.

Leading improvements in careers teaching and learning

Careers education should evoke in students the same kind of excitement and pleasure that they experience from the best teaching in other areas of the curriculum. 'Routine' careers education is characterized as follows:

- Uninspiring, e.g. repetitive practising of how to complete a CV with no skill development
- Lacking in challenge, e.g. mundane worksheet activities that students know will not be checked
- Procedural, e.g. telling students how to apply for things which allows the urgent (i.e. meeting the deadline) to drive out the important (e.g. what values are important to you in your career?)
- Negative, e.g. holding the threat of unemployment over students' heads instead of enthusing them with the prospect of finding meaningful and fulfilling careers
- Driven by a narrow agenda, e.g. when the programme focuses on employability rather than students' wider personal and economic well-being.

One of the ways to raise standards is to apply quality criteria that focus attention on outcomes for learners. Table 7.2 shows how the generic criteria used to assess the quality of teaching by Ofsted, the inspection agency for schools in England, can be applied to careers teaching. The effective practice column gives our examples of what outstanding careers teaching might look like. It may not be possible to demonstrate all these characteristics in an individual lesson, but they should be discernible over time.

Table 7.2 Outstanding careers teaching

Ofsted criteria (2012)	Examples of effective practice
Teaching leads to progress	• Nearly all learners, including individuals with special needs, make sustained progress (see Chapter 2 for examples of how to observe progress). • Teaching approaches are matched to intended outcomes, e.g. collaborative learning is used to teach about interdependence in working life. • When outside speakers contribute to careers education, the teacher evaluates their impact on students' learning. • Teachers have expert subject knowledge and skills.
High expectations	• Teachers have equally high expectations of the quality of work that students will do in careers lessons as they have in other subjects. • Teachers expect students to have realistically high aspirations regardless of their socio-economic circumstances. • Teachers provide the right amount of challenge and support to enable students to develop and test their career thinking. • Students are expected to take increasing responsibility for the direction of their own careers and for managing the influences on them.

(Continued)

Table 7.2 (Continued)

Ofsted criteria (2012)	Examples of effective practice
Students' learning	• Students are active participants in their own learning. • The teacher takes into account students' current knowledge and understanding. • Students have trust in each other and exhibit a high level of personal, social and emotional skills so that they can safely discuss sensitive and controversial career issues. • Learning is relevant to students' current needs and builds on their previous experiences. • Learning is set within the context of a broad and balanced framework of worthwhile career learning outcomes.
Checking of understanding	• Teachers check students' understanding throughout lessons and make helpful interventions where necessary. • Students' thinking is challenged through effective questioning by the teacher.
General attainment in Mathematics and English	• Careers teaching promotes literacy and numeracy skills (linked to employability) and is clearly part of a whole-school strategy to raise attainment in English and Maths.
Climate for learning	• Teaching is imaginative and lively. • Students feel that their contributions to the lesson are genuinely valued. • The climate for learning generates a positive work ethic based on intrinsic motivation to learn.
Assessment for learning	• Students are adept at self-assessment and peer assessment. • The teacher takes into account students' previous attainment and progress. • The teacher gives students feedback on how to improve. (For more on assessment for learning, see Chapter 2.)
Pupils' needs met	• Extension activities are provided for students who need them. Similarly, additional support is provided for those who need it to progress, e.g. for students with literacy problems.
Behaviour and attitude to learning	• Time on task is high, and students are visibly immersed in their own learning. • The teacher's strong and consistent approach to behaviour management creates an exceptionally positive climate for learning. • Improvements in behaviour over time are noticeable for individuals or groups with particular behaviour needs.

This checklist can be used to observe careers teaching. When carrying out an observation, it is important to adhere to the school policy and procedures on lesson observations.

Facilitating the professional learning of all staff

The leader for CLD can actively encourage the professional learning of all staff involved in providing CLD opportunities for students. In collaboration with the school leader for professional learning, the leader can undertake a training needs analysis either by administering a short questionnaire survey or by meetings with key curriculum and pastoral leaders. When doing the analysis, it is worth remembering the following points:

• This is an opportunity to inform staff about the scope and value of CLD which may be new to them.

- Carrying out an analysis raises expectations among staff that their needs will be met. How this is managed is important for the future cooperation and goodwill of staff.
- The areas of questioning need to strike a balance between asking staff what support they need to develop and improve something they already do and asking them to do something new. It is also very important that consensus or agreement has been reached about any new activities that are being proposed, e.g. through the school development planning process.
- Staff are busy, and so if you want a good response, keep the survey short and straight-forward to answer. A mix of structured questions (e.g. 'Do you need help with directing students to sources of information about local apprenticeship opportunities?') and more open-ended questions (e.g. 'What other help would you like?') is useful.

The strategies for meeting the needs that have been identified are likely to involve a mix of self-help and formal training activities. The range could include the following:

- Asking for student feedback
- Observing others
- Holding learning conversations in the school or across a network of schools
- Reading articles and reports
- Joint planning
- Team teaching
- Creating a careers area on the staff VLE where staff can find and share resources and engage in professional debate
- Establishing a professional library (print and online)
- Doing action research in the classrooms
- Participating in an action learning set or a professional learning community, especially if it is based on self-help principles
- Having a mentor or coach
- Participating in the school's internal professional learning programme
- Accessing external courses in school via webinars and e-learning, with the possibility of accreditation.

A key priority is to create a positive climate for professional learning related to careers. This can be accomplished in the following ways:

- Providing high-quality, ready-made resources that will make their jobs easier, especially useful if it helps staff with something they have to do anyway, e.g. by preparing a hand-out on how to conduct target-setting interviews with students.
- Facilitating 'quick wins' and 'early rewards' for innovators. Success encourages persistence, e.g. helping a subject department to plan a themed learning day with the involvement of local employers will encourage other departments to repeat and develop work-related learning activities.
- Making CLD fun and challenging for staff so that they will do the same for their students, e.g. arrange a career coaching session for staff to help them plan their careers, make good applications and prepare for interviews.
- Making the session active or interactive, e.g. by getting staff to do the activity they will do later with students.

- Signalling the importance of the activity by ensuring that members of the senior leadership team participate as well, e.g. if you arrange for groups of staff to visit local universities, training providers or businesses to update their knowledge, make sure that the senior leadership team participate as well.
- Harnessing informal networks, e.g. encouraging staff who get on well with each other to work together
- Being realistic about how change happens, e.g. recognising that some staff will be slower than others to adopt new approaches.
- Scheduling inputs at regular meetings (e.g. staff meetings and staff conferences) rather than arranging additional meetings.
- Making sure that staff do not come to professional learning sessions 'cold', e.g. by sending out a briefing paper beforehand with possible discussion questions on it.
- Taking part in the induction programme for new staff.

Organising a professional learning event

The following elements are the keys to organising a successful event.

Planning

Establish the intended outcomes by carrying out consumer research so that you have a clearer notion of what participants are expecting to gain from the event. These become your priorities and make it easier to decide what to include and what to leave out. Don't overlook what you want to achieve for yourself.

Administration

Colleagues appreciate sound organisation. This involves choosing suitable accommodation, ensuring the equipment needed is available, publicising the event well and providing welcome refreshments. Keeping to time is essential.

Delivery

Give particular attention to the beginning and end of the session. Think how you will grab people's attention at the start and close the session on a positive note. Variety, touches of humour and appropriate changes of pace will help to keep the attention of the audience. Aim for an appropriate balance of inputs and activities. Where possible, engage the interest of colleagues by structuring the content so that they become active thinkers rather than passive listeners. Remember how difficult it is to pay full attention for more than 20 minutes.

Evaluation

Evaluation can take place through the leader's observation of body language, the level of interest and commitment shown during the activities and the quality of thinking revealed through the activities. In the final plenary, you can organise verbal feedback through card rounds, structured reflection in pairs and small groups and open-ended questions. Written evaluation pro formas can give participants the opportunity to provide satisfaction ratings and commit themselves to follow-up action (e.g. list two actions you will undertake as a result of your participation in today's event).

Record keeping

Effective record keeping is a vital part of the leadership and management of CLD. The key purposes are as follows:

- Maintaining operations. A CLD calendar will enable you to keep track of upcoming events in the school's CLD programme as well as to remind you of deadlines and renewal dates, e.g. the date of the next revision of the school policy for CLD.
- Managing resources. A contacts database is a very useful way of recording offers of help from parents, local employers and other school partners.
- Costing provision and making decisions about the deployment of resources. Record keeping can help provide the evidence needed to make decisions about overall levels of resourcing required and how those resources are deployed. Useful records include the following:

  o   A calendar to help CLD staff manage their time and to see where pressure points occur in the year
  o   A financial spreadsheet showing areas of expenditure
  o   Registers of attendance and participation to show the demand and take-up of services that the CLD team provide such as lunchtime drop-in sessions, individual interviews, small-group work and careers lessons
  o   Counts and estimates of the time spent on digital communications and services, e.g. emails sent and answered, tweets, blogs, website updates.

Monitoring student attainment, progress and destinations

Record keeping helps the school to keep track of students' attainment and progress. It enables the school to target support more effectively, especially where a number of staff are involved in helping the same student.

Good practice in record keeping emphasises the following points:

- Records should be confidential and only used for the purposes that the student agreed.
- Students and their parents should be able to see any records that you have created.
- You should not collect or keep unnecessary information about the student.
- Out of date and inaccurate information on a student should be destroyed.

Recording systems can be paper-based and/or computer-based. The two main groups of records are as follows:

- Personal or individual records, e.g. information on a particular student such as their interview discussion notes
- Group records, e.g. information on the year group such as their participation in the activities in the careers programme.

Table 7.3 Types of personal career records

Types of personal records	Their uses
Careers registration form	Ask students to fill out a careers registration form and keep a copy for themselves. This will help you to get ready to interview them individually or to put them into groups for careers education activities. An example of a template for a registration form is shown subsequently.
Interview discussion notes	These are notes made during an interview with the student. They are particularly useful for recording follow-up actions which you and/or the student have agreed to take. Remember to give students a copy for themselves and their parents/carers.
Personal profile	The personal profile summarises the qualities, skills, interests, values, etc. of the student. It can assist the process of helping students to match themselves to particular opportunities in education or employment
Assessment tests and questionnaires	The reports or printouts from aptitude tests, interest questionnaires, problem checklists, etc. can help you to offer appropriate career guidance
Plans	Plans contain a record of students' goals and the course of action they propose to take to help them achieve those goals. Plans can be for different purposes, e.g. action plans (short term), development plans (medium and long term) or change plans (to make progress and manage transitions in their lives).

Table 7.3 summarises different types of personal records and their uses. Records can be stored in students' careers portfolios if they have them (see Chapter 2).

Careers registration form

First name and surname

Tutor/house group

Date of birth

Mobile phone number

Email address

Health – do you have any health issues that could affect your career choice? Please indicate if you are not sure, or leave blank if you would rather not say.

Subjects and examinations you are taking currently

Name of subject	Qualification to be gained (where applicable)

Public examination results

Date	Qualifications gained, including names of subjects	Grade

Work experience (Record any experience of work, e.g. work placements, part-time jobs, voluntary work.)

Dates	What did you do?	Name of organisation/provider of the opportunity

Recent achievements

```


```

Skills (List your main skills. Underline your top five skills. Put an asterisk against those which you would like to develop further.)

```


```

Leisure interests (What do you do in your spare time that an interviewer/recruiter would like to know about you?)

```


```

Career ideas (Mention up to three main ideas.)

Do you have any job or career ideas at the moment? What are they?	Why do you think this choice might suit you?

Current goals and plans (Mention anything that you are doing now towards your career, e.g. volunteering, applying for part-time jobs.)

```


```

Careers advice received (If you have spoken to other people about your career ideas or completed any questionnaires – computer- or paper-based – what did you find out?)

From a careers specialist
From other people (including family)

Careers help required (What information or advice, if anything, are you looking for at the moment?)

```


```

Today's date

```


```

Developing a communications strategy

The long-term goals of a strategy to improve communications include the following:

- Building awareness of the scope and purpose of the school's CLD provision
- Helping those who use the provision to access it more efficiently
- Making more effective use of resources
- Engaging other members of the school community in providing and developing the school's CLD provision.

Developing your role as a communicator has a key bearing on your style of leadership of CLD. The following are pitfalls to avoid:

- Overloading people with too much information
- 'Telling' people when the situation requires 'consulting' with them
- Passing on advertising and marketing information about career opportunities when people expect you to provide impartial information
- Overcommitting yourself and not being able to maintain all the channels of communication that you have established.

Channels of communication between the CLD team and students, their families, staff, employers and the wider community are a vital part of publicising the services you provide, raising the profile of CLD and for getting feedback on it. Social media and networking have made possible new and more spontaneous ways of interacting with the groups you want to reach.

A first step is to do a review of the effectiveness of your current communications with different groups. With regard to parents and carers, for example, what have your communications been about and how did you communicate with them? You may have tried some or all of the following ways of communicating with them:

- Talking and adding meaning by using voice and body language
- Letters home
- Articles in parents' newsletter/e-newsletter
- Questionnaires (given out at parents' evenings or posted online)
- Posters and displays (including plasma screens)
- Presentations and discussions at parents meetings
- Reports on progress and attainment
- Leaflets and booklets
- Individual consultations
- Careers pages on the school website/VLE
- Blogs, texts, tweets.

You can interrogate your approach to communicating with parents and carers (or any of the groups you communicate with) by asking yourself the following questions:

- Was this communication necessary?
- What was I trying to achieve by it?

- Was this communication transmitted in the best way, or would a different type of communication have worked better?
- How productive was it?

A review of your communication practices is also an opportunity to identify skills you would like to develop (e.g. effective writing, managing meetings, using social media). You can include any needs you have identified in your professional learning and development plan.

Conclusion

We have now reached the end of this practical guide. In Part I, we focused on preparing to teach CLD, and in Part II, we presented a wide range of ideas for facilitating career resilience, happiness and growth with different age groups. Part III focused on the effective leadership and management of CLD. We hope that you will be keen to try out some of the ideas presented, but more importantly, that these ideas will inspire you to be creative and to try out your own. The importance of preparing young people for life and work cannot be underestimated, and we hope that this guide will enable you to make an important and lasting difference in the lives of young people.

References

Bassot, B. (2006). 'Constructing New Understandings of Career Guidance: Joining the Dots'. In H. L. Reid and J. Bimrose (eds), *Constructing the Future IV: Transforming Career Guidance*. Stourbridge: Institute of Career Guidance (pp. 49–60).

Bassot, B. (2009). 'Career Learning and Development: A Bridge to the Future'. In H. L. Reid (ed.), *Constructing the Future V: Career Guidance for Changing Contexts*. Stourbridge: Institute of Career Guidance (pp. 1–11).

Bimrose, J., Barnes, S. A., and Hughes, D. (2008). 'Adult Career Progression and Advancement: A Five Year Study of the Effectiveness of Guidance'. [Online]. Coventry: Warwick Institute for Employment Research and Department for Education and Skills. Available from http://www2.warwick.ac.uk/fac/soc/ier/publications/2008/eg_report_4_years_on_final .pdf. Accessed 2 May 2013.

Bimrose, J., and Hearne, L. (2012). 'Resilience and Career Adaptability: Qualitative Studies of Adult Career Counselling'. *Journal of Vocational Behavior*, 81(3): 338–344.

Black, P. J., and William, D. (1998). 'Assessment and Classroom Learning'. *Assessment in Education: Principles, Policy and Practice*, 5(1): 7–73.

Bourdieu, P. (1986). 'The Forms of Capital'. In J. Richardson (ed.), *Handbook of Theory and Research for the Sociology of Education*. New York: Greenwood (pp. 241–258).

Bruner, J. (1996). *The Culture of Education*. London: Harvard University Press.

Career Development Institute (CDI). (2012). *The ACEG Framework for Careers and Work-Related Education*. [Online]. Available from http://www.thecdi.net/write/CWRE_User_Guide. pdf. Accessed 30 May 2013.

Coleman, J., and Hagell, A. (2007). *Adolescence, Risk and Resilience: Against the Odds*. Chichester: John Wiley.

Coleman, J. C., and Hendry, L. (1999). *The Nature of Adolescence* (3rd edn). London: Routledge.

Communication 4 All. (n.d.). 'Story Planning'. [Online]. Available from http://www.communication4all.co.uk/http/Story%20Writing.htm. Accessed 11 May 2013.

Corneli, J., and Danoff, C. J. (2011). 'Paragogy'. [Online]. Available from http://ceur-ws.org/ Vol-739/paper_5.pdf. Accessed 29 August 2013.

Csikszentmihályi, M. (1990). *Flow: The Psychology of Optimal Experience*. New York: Harper and Row.

Department for Education (DfE). (2012). 'United Nations Convention on the Rights of the Child'. [Online]. Available from http://www.education.gov.uk/childrenandyoungpeople/ healthandwellbeing/b0074766/uncrc. Accessed 5 June 2013.

Department for Education (DfE). (2013). '2014 National Curriculum'. [Online]. Available from https://www.education.gov.uk/schools/teachingandlearning/curriculum/national curriculum2014. Accessed 29 August 2013.

Department for Education (DfE). (2013). 'Statutory Guidance: The Duty to Secure Independent and Impartial Careers Guidance for Young People in Schools'. [Online]. Available from http://media.education.gov.uk/assets/files/pdf/s/careers%20guidance%20for%20 schools%20-%20statutory%20guidance%20-%20march%202013.pdf. Accessed 30 May 2013.

Donoghue, J. (ed.). (2008). *Better Practice – A Guide to Delivering Effective Career Learning 11–19*. Godalming: AICE/ACEG/CESP.

Erikson, E. H. (1950). *Childhood and Society*. New York: Norton.

Gottfredson, L. (1981). 'Circumscription and Compromise: A Developmental Theory of Occupational Aspirations'. *Journal of Counseling Psychology*, 28(6): 545–579.

Hase, S., and Kenyon, C. (2000). 'From Andragogy to Heutagogy'. [Online]. Available from Ultibase, RMIT, http://ultibase.rmit.edu.au/Articles/dec00/hase2.htm. Accessed 7 June 2013.

Hearne, L. (2010). *Measuring Individual Progression in Adult Guidance: An Irish Case Study*. Waterford: Waterford Institute of Technology.

Herzberg, F., Mausner, B., and Snyderman, B. (1959). *The Motivation to Work* (2nd edn). New York: John Wiley.

Higgins, G. (1994). *Resilient Adults: Overcoming a Cruel Past*. San Francisco, CA: Jossey-Bass.

Hodkinson, P., Sparkes, A., and Hodkinson, H. (1996). *Triumphs and Tears: Young People, Markets and the Transition from School to Work*. London: David Fulton.

Holland, J.L. (1973). Making Vocational Choices: A Theory of Careers. Englewood Cliffs, NJ: Prentice Hall.

Honey, P., and Mumford, A. (2000). *The Learning Styles Helper's Guide*. Maidenhead: Peter Honey Publications.

Howard, K., and Walsh, M. (2011). 'Children's Conceptions of Career Choice and Attainment: Model Development'. *Journal of Career Development*, 38(3): 256–271.

Johnson, C., Marks, S., Matthews, M., and Pike, J. (1987). *Key Skills: Enterprise Skills through Active Learning*. London: Hodder and Stoughton.

Kahneman, D., Krueger, A., Schkade, D., Schwarz, N., and Stone, A. (2006). 'Would You Be Happier If You Were Richer? A Focusing Illusion'. *Science*, 312(5782): 1908–1910

Keyes, C., Shmotkin, D., and Ryff, C. (2002). 'Optimizing Well-Being: The Empirical Encounter of Two Traditions'. *Journal of Personality and Social Psychology*, 82: 1007–1022.

Kolb, D. (1984) *Experiential Learning: Experience as the Source of Learning and Development*. Englewood Cliffs, NJ: Prentice Hall.

Landsberger, H. A. (1958). *Hawthorne Revisited*. Ithaca, NY: Cornell University.

Learning and Skills Improvement Service (LSIS). (2012). *A Guide to the Blueprint for Careers and Its Implementation*. [Online]. Available from http://repository.excellencegateway.org .uk/fedora/objects/eg:2130/datastreams/DOC/content. Accessed 21 April 2013.

Luft, J., and Ingham, H. (1955). 'The Johari Window, a Graphic Model of Interpersonal Awareness'. Available from http://www.businessballs.com/johariwindowmodel.htm. Accessed 5 September 2013.

Maslow, A. (1954). *Motivation and Personality*. New York: Harper.

Office for Standards in Education (Ofsted). (2012). *Measuring Happiness: A Consultation with Children from Care and Children Living in Residential and Boarding Schools. Reported by the Children's Rights Director for England*. [Online]. Available from http://www.ofsted.gov.uk/ resources/measuring-happiness. Accessed 7 June 2013.

Patton, W., and McMahon, M. (2006). 'The Systems Theory Framework of Career Development and Counseling: Connecting Theory and Practice'. *International Journal for the Advancement of Counselling*, 28(2): 153–166.

Peterson, G. W., Rollins, B. C., and Thomas, D. L. (1985). 'Parental Influence and Adolescent Conformity: Compliance and Internalisation'. *Youth in Society*, 16(4): 397–420.

Poilpot, M.-P. (1999). *Un Nouvel Âge de la Vie: le Temps de la Postadolescence*. Ramonville Saint-Agne: Fondation pour l'enfance.

Prospects. (2005). *The Real Game*. [Online]. Available from http://www.realgame.co.uk/. Accessed 13 May 2013.

Pryor, R., and Bright, J. (2011). *The Chaos Theory of Careers*. London: Routledge.

Putnam, R. D. (2000). *Bowling Alone: The Collapse and Revival of American Community*. New York: Simon and Schuster.

ResearchBods. (2012). 'Parent Power Dominates Education Choices' on behalf of the Chartered Institute of Public Relations (CIPR) Education & Skills Group. [Online]. Available from http://newsroom.cipr.co.uk/parent-power-dominates-education-choices/. Accessed 5 June 2013.

Rowe, N., Wilkin, A., and Wilson, R. (2012). *Mapping of Seminal Reports on Good Teaching* (NFER Research Programme: Developing the Education Workforce). Slough: NFER.

Savickas, M. L. (2005). 'The Theory and Practice of Career Construction'. In R. W. Lent and S. D. Brown (eds), *Career Development and Counseling: Putting Theory and Research to Work*. Hoboken, NJ: John Wiley & Sons (pp. 42–70).

Savickas, M. L., and Hartung, P. J. (2012). *My Career Story: An Autobiographical Workbook for Life-Career Success*. Available from http://www.vocopher.com. Accessed 29 August 2013.

Savickas, M. L., and Porfeli, E. J. (2012). 'Career Adapt-Abilities Scale: Construction, Reliability and Measurement Equivalence across 13 Countries'. *Journal of Vocational Behavior*, 80(3): 661–763.

Siemens, G. (2004). 'A Learning Theory for the Digital Age'. [Online]. Available from http://www.elearnspace.org/Articles/connectivism.htm. Accessed 17 May 2013.

Smith, W. J., Howard, J. T., and Harrington, K. V. (2005). 'Essential Formal Mentor Characteristics and Functions in Governmental and Non-governmental Organizations from the Program Administrator's and the Mentor's Perspective'. *Public Personnel Management*, 34(1): 31–58.

Treseder, P. (1997). *Empowering Children and Young People: Training Manual*. London: Save the Children and Children's Rights Office.

Tuckman, B. W., and Jensen, M.A.C. (1977). 'Stages of Small Group Development Revisited'. *Group and Organizational Studies*, 2: 419–427.

Turnbull, J. (2009). *Coaching for Learning: A Practical Guide for Encouraging Learning*. London: Continuum.

van Hoorn, A., and Maseland, R. (2013). 'Does a Protestant Work Ethic Exist? Evidence from the Well-Being Effect of Unemployment'. *Journal of Economic Behavior & Organization*, 91: 1–12.

Warr, P. (2007). *Work, Happiness and Unhappiness*. Mahwah, NJ: Lawrence Erlbaum Associates.

Wolin, S. J., and Wolin, S. (1993). *The Resilient Self: How Survivors of Troubled Families Survive against Adversity*. New York: Villard.

Wood, D. (1998). *How Children Think and Learn* (2nd edn). Oxford: Blackwell.

Index

ACEG framework 42–5, 52–3, 68, 84, 100, 103
active learning 7, 16, 30–1, 35, 113
assessment 19, 33–4, 38, 40, 42, 51, 52–3, 113, 117

Bassot, B. 5
Bimrose, J., Barnes, S.A. and Hughes, D. 11, 12, 90
Bimrose, J. and Hearne, L. 11
Black, P.J. and William, D. 33
Bourdieu, P. 46
Bruner, J. 15

career: adaptability 11; growth 6, 7, 8, 9, 15–17, 41, 70–3, 86–9, 101–4; guidance 5, 18–19, 108, 109, 117; happiness 6, 7, 8, 9, 12–15, 41, 65–70, 79–86, 95–101; narrative 15, 21, 39, 70–1, 86–7, 101–2; resilience 6, 7, 8, 9–12, 41, 59–65, 74–9, 90–5
careers lead team 107–10
CLD bridge model 5, 6–8, 9
Coleman, J. and Hagell, A. 10, 76
Coleman, J. C. and Hendry, L. 90, 92
collaborative approaches 19, 27, 29, 42, 46–8, 112
communications strategy 120–1
cooperative learning 18, 30, 31–2, 40
Corneli, J. and Danoff, C. J. 27
curriculum planning 47, 48

digital technology 27, 28–9
Donoghue, J. 54

EFFE 8–9, 49
enquiry-based learning 26–7
Erikson, E. H. 74
experiential learning 20, 32–3

flow 13, 14, 18, 20, 53

Gottfredson, L. 59

Hase, S. and Kenyon, C. 27
Hearne, L. 11
Herzberg, F., Mausner, B. and Snyderman, B. 83
Higgins, G. 10, 76
Hodkinson, P., Sparkes, A. and Hodkinson, H. 20
Honey, P. and Mumford, A. 26
Hoorn, A. van, and Maseland, R. 99
Howard, K. and Walsh, M. 59, 90

interactive learning 8, 19, 27–30, 114

Johnson, C., Marks, S., Matthews, M., and Pike, J. 84, 96

Kahneman, D., Krueger, A., Schkade, D., Schwarz, N., and Stone, A. 78
Keyes, C., Shmotkin, D., and Ryff, C. 12
Kolb, D. 32

labour market demands 3, 4, 5, 7, 10, 43, 46, 48, 51–3, 59, 76–7, 109
Landsberger, H. A. 83
learners' needs 46
lesson plans 41, 51, 53–4, 108
lifelong learning 7, 15
Luft, J., and Ingham, H. 24

Maslow, A. 97
monitoring, review and evaluation 41, 49–51, 111

networks 18, 27, 44, 46, 47, 62–3, 115

Ofsted 66, 112–13

pastoral support 34–6, 77, 113
Patton, W., and McMahon, M. 90

Peterson, G. W., Rollins, B. C., and Thomas, D. L. 59
Poilpot. M.-P. 10
policy 107, 110–11, 113, 116
portfolios 21–4, 28, 39, 68, 117
problem-based learning 7, 26
Pryor, R., and Bright, J. 18
Putnam, R. D. 46

record keeping 116–20
resources 29, 30, 41, 48, 61, 108, 109, 111, 114, 116, 120
Rowe, N., Wilkin, A., and Wilson, R. 19

Savickas, M. L. 18; and Hartung, P. J. 22; and Porfeli, E. J. 12
schemes of work 41, 51, 108
Siemens, G. 27
Smith, W. J., Howard, J. T., and Harrington, K. V. 91

staff development 111
student involvement 54–6

teaching approaches 18, 19, 20–33, 40, 112
tests and questionnaires 24–5, 38, 117
Treseder, P. 56
Tuckman, B. W., and Jensen, M.A.C. 32
Turnbull, J. 20
tutorial model 35–6

Warr, P. 83
well-being 4, 5, 7, 12, 13, 14, 19, 42, 45, 61, 68, 81, 84, 96, 97, 98, 99, 100, 101, 102
Wolin, S. J., and Wolin, S. 11, 12
Wood, D. 15

Zone of Proximal Development (ZPD) 15–17, 20, 34, 35–6, 71–2, 87–8, 102–3